MARVELLOUS
= MEALS WITH =
MINCE

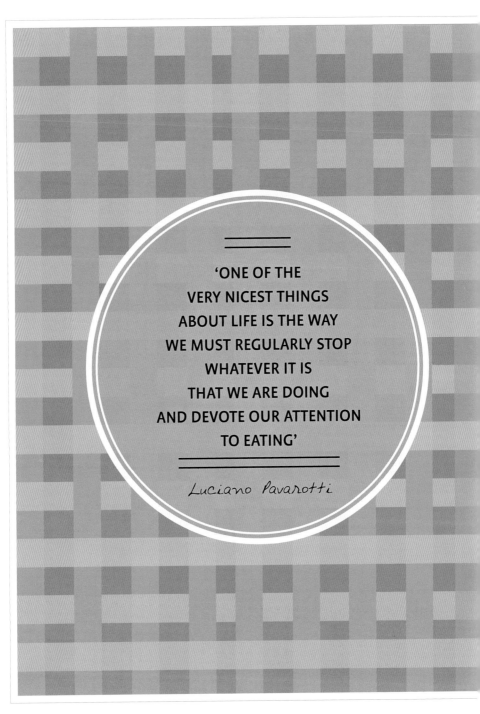

'ONE OF THE
VERY NICEST THINGS
ABOUT LIFE IS THE WAY
WE MUST REGULARLY STOP
WHATEVER IT IS
THAT WE ARE DOING
AND DEVOTE OUR ATTENTION
TO EATING'

Luciano Pavarotti

JOSCELINE DIMBLEBY

MARVELLOUS
= MEALS WITH =
MINCE

PHOTOGRAPHS BY STEVEN JOYCE

Quadrille
PUBLISHING

First published in 2012 by
Quadrille Publishing Limited
Alhambra House
27–31 Charing Cross Road
London WC2H OLS
www.quadrille.co.uk

Editorial Director: Jane O'Shea
Creative Director: Helen Lewis
Editor: Louise McKeever
Designers: Nicola Davidson, Ros Holder
Photographer: Steven Joyce
Food stylist: Xenia von Oswald, assisted by Amelia Holmwood
Production Director: Vincent Smith
Production Controller: Leonie Kellman

Cataloguing in Publication Data: a catalogue record for this book
is available from the British Library.

ISBN 978 184949 150 1

Printed and bound in China.

CONTENTS

Towards the end of the 1970s Sainsbury's made what proved to be an era-changing decision: to start publishing small paperback cookery books that would be sold at the checkout in their stores. They asked me to write the first one – as a trial I suppose – and in 1978 I produced *Cooking for Christmas*, at a time when there were no other Christmas recipe books around. The book sold well and I was asked to follow it quickly with more. After four more in 3 years I was wondering which area of food to work on next, so I asked Sainsbury's what ingredient they sold most of. 'Mince' was the brief but emphatic reply.

It was now the start of the 1980s and England was in the grip of a recession – families were feeling the pinch. However, the prospect of tackling mundane mince didn't depress me, in fact it inspired me. Mince should never be thought of as dull; it is an incredibly versatile ingredient, a true chameleon that combines well with almost any other ingredient and flavouring. As a young music student the first dish I made was a Shepherd's pie and I couldn't resist adding some cumin and coriander. Ever since, the thing I enjoy most about cooking is creativity, a combination of invention and improvisation. So mince was a welcome subject for me. Not just minced beef; I used minced lamb, pork, veal, chicken and turkey as well. And chopped fish – as I could never resist really good fishcakes or feather-light mousse mixtures. The result was *Marvellous Meals with Mince*, which became a bestseller, reprinted eight times between 1982–89; even today, at literary festivals, there are unfailingly people in my audiences who bring battered, food-stained copies of the book for me to sign.

All over the world, as far back as records go, dishes made with chopped meat and fish have been popular. Almost any country you can think of has its own mince recipes, which have often become national dishes: France has steak tartare, Italy has Bolognese, Spain has albondigas, Germany is said to be where the meatloaf originated, America has hamburgers, South Africa has bobotie, Mexico has chilli con carne, Greece has moussaka, Turkey, Iran and India have all manner of delicious kofte and minced kebabs. In North Africa, the Middle East, Asia and the Far East there are countless exquisite dishes made with minced or chopped meat, chicken or fish. Nearer to home Scotland has haggis and England of course has Shepherd's pie, which – unless it is the grey watery affair of my schooldays – is one of our great comfort foods.

Today the meatball seems to be all the rage; from wintry ones in rich sauces to spicy ones which can be grilled on a barbecue in summer, their tantalising aroma wafting into the warm air. But further possibilities with mince are no less pleasurable; mince can be fried, baked, roasted, poached, stewed or grilled, producing a stunning variety of results. It can be used as a filling for pies of all kinds, in mouthwatering sauces for pasta, with noodles or rice, for an enhancing stuffing to put within vegetables, meat, poultry and fish. And, something I find most exciting of all and never tire of experimenting with – the mince itself can be stuffed with a surprise centre.

Crucial to the success of mince dishes is very definite flavouring, which the mince absorbs so well that it can take on any character you choose to give it. Herbs and spices are a natural addition, onions and garlic invaluable, tomatoes hard to do without. Chopped spinach gives moisture and colour, and cheese blends beautifully, either incorporated into the mixture or as a luscious sauce. For a pie topping mashed celeriac, sweet potato, parsnip and swede can be substituted for or mixed with potato. With mince you never run out of new combinations to try.

Yet another virtue of mince is, importantly, economy. What with stuffings, toppings, crusts, and the incorporation of breadcrumbs, root vegetables, pasta or rice you can stretch mince-based dishes to feed an indeterminate number; it is an inexpensive main ingredient which can always be expanded to feed last minute guests. People have told me that they used to give this book to their children when they went to university in order to encourage them to eat affordably but well. One woman, who gave a copy to her son, said that it transformed him from a puny, fussy eating child to a big healthy man for whom cooking was a joy. My son Henry is just such a man, and often uses my recipes in his Leon restaurants.

Young children love mince – partly because they don't have to chew too much – so it's a good way to get them used to new flavours that they profess to find 'yukky', and it's ideal for all age family occasions which include the oldest grandparents who don't dare chew too hard either! The first edition of this book was written when my own children were young; as I started to revise it specific meals and moments came back to me – I remembered tastes, textures, smells, and the appreciative reactions of my children, family and friends as they tried my experimental dishes for the first time.

Now my children have children of their own, who I hope will benefit from the recipes I devised for their parents as children, while adults will see from this varied collection that with very little effort mince can also become a sophisticated dish fit for a party. While working through my first edition, updating the original recipes to profit from a wider choice of ingredients available today, adding extra ideas and a few new recipes, I felt sure it was time to enjoy some more 'marvellous meals with mince'.

Josceline Dimbleby
London, February 2012

BEEF

MYMOTHER'S
• STEAKTARTARE •

- 8 tbsp mayonnaise
- 2–3 shallots, finely chopped
- a handful of flat-leaf parsley, finely chopped
- 2–3 tsp capers, finely chopped
- freshly ground black pepper
- mixed salad leaves
- 500g extra lean freshly minced beef

SERVES 4

It is comforting to be able to remember my mother telling me, with her wonderful laugh and sparkling eyes, about this personalised version of steak tartare. She had a great enthusiasm for cooking and I love her idea of incorporating a flavoured mayonnaise instead of raw egg yolks into the meat. Only use very fresh, and never frozen, beef for this dish.

Place the mayonnaise in a mixing bowl and stir in the shallots, parsley, capers and some pepper. Arrange the salad leaves on four serving plates. Just before serving mix the beef thoroughly into the mayonnaise mixture. Shape into patties or spoon the mince mixture onto the salad leaves and serve.

LETTUCE PARCELS
· STUFFED ᴡⁱᵗʰ PAPRIKA BEEF ·

- 50g basmati or long grain rice
- sea salt and freshly ground black pepper
- 2 tbsp sunflower oil
- 1 red onion, chopped
- 2 large garlic cloves, finely chopped
- 1 tbsp paprika
- 500g lean beef mince
- 3 fresh plum tomatoes, chopped into cubes
- 4 pinches of mild chilli powder
- 2 tsp caster sugar
- 1 large cos lettuce or Savoy cabbage
- 1 tbsp sherry vinegar
- 4 tbsp extra virgin olive oil
- 1 rounded tsp wholegrain mustard

SERVES 6

You might not think it but cos lettuce is excellent briefly cooked. For this recipe I blanch the leaves so that they can be stuffed with paprika beef, tomatoes and onions; it is an unusual and delicious dish for a summer lunch, or as part of a cold buffet. As an alternative to the lettuce I often use Savoy cabbage leaves which take a bit longer to go limp.

Cook the rice in salted water until just tender, drain and set aside. Heat the sunflower oil in a large frying pan. Add the onion and fry over a gentle heat until softened. Stir in the garlic, paprika and the beef. Increase the heat and stir with a wooden spoon to separate and brown the meat. Mix in the chopped tomatoes and continue cooking for 7–12 minutes, or until the tomatoes are soft and any juices have evaporated. Stir in the chilli powder and sugar. Remove from the heat, add in the cooked rice and thoroughly combine. Set aside and leave until cold.

Separate and wash the lettuce leaves, cutting away any thick stalk from the bottom of the larger leaves. Bring a large saucepan of salted water to the boil and plunge in the whole leaves for a minute or less, just until softened. Drain the leaves, lay them out separately on a flat surface and pat with absorbent kitchen paper to dry thoroughly. Spoon a good amount of the mince mixture onto the middle of each lettuce leaf and wrap the leaves around the filling to create little parcels. Lay them join-side down in a shallow serving dish. Just before serving mix together the vinegar, olive oil, mustard and seasoning in a small bowl and pour over the lettuce parcels.

HOMEMADE
• BURGERS •

- 500g lean, coarsely minced fresh beef
- 50g rindless smoked bacon, finely chopped
- 2 tsp small capers (optional)
- 2 tsp chilli powder
- sea salt
- sunflower oil
- 4 burger buns
- 75g Saint Agur or other blue cheese (optional)

SERVES 4

I'll never forget my first real taste of hamburgers – as they were called then – when I first went to America as a young newlywed in the 1960s. With juicy beef, pink in the middle and charred on the outside, they were a world away from the thin grey circles of something that were known as hamburgers in England at that time. Now things are different, but homemade burgers still taste the best, particularly in the summer when you can cook them on a barbecue for the perfect charred flavour. I give them smokiness and depth by adding smoked bacon and capers. Serve in hot seedy buns with a leafy green salad.

Put the beef, bacon, capers (if using) and chilli powder into a bowl and mix together thoroughly using a wooden spoon. Season with a little salt.

Divide the mixture into four and pat firmly into flattened circles about 1cm thick and the circumference of your buns. Cover each burger in a little oil. Heat your grill to its highest setting and put the burgers high up under it.

Grill for barely 2 minutes on each side – the outside should be speckled dark brown to black and the inside, crucially, should still be pink and succulent. Meanwhile, cut the buns in half and lightly toast them.

To make this a deliciously tangy cheeseburger, crumble the cheese on top of each hot burger as you place it between the buns. Eat at once, of course.

OVEN
· CHEESEBURGERS ·

- 500g lean beef mince
- a small handful of flat-leaf parsley, finely chopped
- sea salt and freshly ground black pepper
- 4 wholemeal or seeded baps
- 75g Gruyére or Jarlsberg cheese, grated

SERVES 4

Here is surely the simplest way to make cheeseburgers. This method is especially useful for an easy children's supper or picnic. The meat remains soft and juicy in the centre and the cheese melts into the meat as it cooks.

Place the beef mince into a bowl and, using a wooden spoon, mix in the parsley and some salt and pepper. Cut the baps in half. Split the mince into four equal parts and roughly shape into burgers. Roughly press the mince onto the bottom of each bap. Divide the grated cheese into four and press on top of the meat. Top with the other half of each bap and wrap individually in foil.

Preheat the oven to 240°C/Gas mark 9. Place the foil parcels onto a baking tray and cook towards the top of the oven for 15–20 minutes, depending on how rare you like your beef to be.

BEEF <small>AND</small> ONION
• FLATBREADS •

INGREDIENTS

- 350g beef mince
- 1 large red onion, very finely chopped
- ½–1 tsp mild chilli powder
- sea salt
- 350g wholemeal flour, plus extra for dusting
- 150ml water
- groundnut or sunflower oil, for frying

SERVES 5–6

These are a bit like wholemeal pancakes and make a really simple dish that goes well with a salad. My children used to love them for supper and even though I tried to dissuade him, my son Henry used to smother his in tomato ketchup. During the summer we sometimes ate them cold, wrapped around salad leaves and slices of tomato.

In a large bowl, mix together the mince and onion and season with the chilli powder and a generous sprinkling of salt. Add the flour and mix together using your hands. Gradually stir in the water, using just enough to make the mixture stick together.

Knead on a floured board for 3–4 minutes, or until smooth and pliable. Then take handfuls of the dough and shape into balls, they should be a little smaller than tennis balls. Roll each ball out as thinly as you can, sprinkling both the board and the rolling pin with plenty of flour to prevent sticking.

Fill a large, heavy frying pan with oil to about a 5mm depth and fry the breads one by one over a medium to high heat, turning once to brown on each side. Place on absorbent kitchen paper to drain any excess oil and pile on a serving dish. Keep them warm in a low oven until ready to serve.

BEEF AND MUSHROOM
· RISSOLES ·

INGREDIENTS

- 500g beef mince
- 1 onion, coarsely grated
- a bunch of flat-leaf parsley, finely chopped
- 1 egg, lightly beaten
- 100g chestnut mushrooms, finely chopped
- sea salt and freshly ground black pepper
- 1 tbsp olive oil

For the sauce:
- 500g fresh plum tomatoes
- 50g butter
- 1 red onion, thinly sliced into rings
- 2 large garlic cloves, finely chopped
- 2 tsp caster sugar
- sea salt and freshly ground black pepper

SERVES 4–5

I always think of a true rissole as being oblong shaped and covered in crunchy breadcrumbs, but I call these rissoles because they can't quite be classified as meatballs. For convenience they can be prepared in advance and kept warm in the oven for hours – perfect for fitting in with a hectic family's comings and goings. Delicious served with peas, broccoli and new potatoes.

Put the beef into a bowl and knead with dampened hands for a few minutes until soft. Add the onion, half the parsley and the beaten egg. Mix together with a wooden spoon, stir in the mushrooms and season with some salt and plenty of pepper. Form the mixture into ping-pong sized balls.

Heat the olive oil in a large frying pan and fry the balls over a high heat for a few minutes, just to brown them, turning carefully once or twice. Remove from the heat.

To make the sauce, make a small incision in the tomatoes and place in a bowl. Cover with boiling water and leave for a minute. Drain, remove and discard the skin and finely chop the flesh. Heat the butter in a large, heavy saucepan and add the chopped tomatoes, onion and garlic. Cover the pan and leave to simmer gently for 8–10 minutes, or until the tomatoes are very soft and mushy. Stir in the sugar and season to taste with salt and pepper.

Spoon the rissoles into the tomato sauce together with any juices from the pan. Cover and simmer very gently for 20 minutes. Sprinkle with the remaining parsley and serve straight from the pan.

OPEN PIE WITH GARLIC AND HERB PASTRY

INGREDIENTS

- 1 tbsp groundnut or sunflower oil
- 500g lean beef mince
- 1 large garlic clove, finely chopped
- 225g chicory, roughly chopped
- sea salt and freshly ground black pepper
- 2 eggs, plus 1 egg yolk, lightly whisked
- 300ml whole milk
- 100g Cheddar or hard goat's cheese, grated

For the pastry:
- 100g butter, plus extra for greasing
- 225g plain flour
- 2 large garlic cloves, roughly chopped
- 1 tsp sea salt
- 1 rounded tsp dried oregano
- 1 tbsp tomato purée
- 2 tbsp water
- freshly ground black pepper

SERVES 6

I first made this open pie when I was experimenting with using an easy butter and water pastry method. It is a good family and friends dish for the weekend – a delicious mingling of tastes that all ages will enjoy.

Lightly butter a 18cm loose-based, deep cake tin. To make the pastry, sift the flour into a bowl. Crush the garlic and salt to a purée using a pestle and mortar and place in a saucepan with the oregano, butter, tomato purée, water and pepper. Cook until the butter has melted and pour into the flour. Stir with a wooden spoon to make a smooth dough. Take pieces of the dough and use your fingers to evenly line the tin. Press the dough up the sides and just over the edge. Refrigerate for 30 minutes while you prepare the filling.

Heat the oil in a large frying pan over a high heat. Add the mince and stir until separated and browned. Mix in the garlic and chicory and cook for 4–5 minutes. Remove from the heat, season and set to one side.

Preheat the oven to 200°C/Gas mark 6. Lightly fork the bottom of the pastry and bake blind for 20 minutes. Remove from the oven and lower the heat to 170°C/Gas mark 3. Place the eggs in a bowl. Heat the milk in a saucepan until just boiling and pour over the eggs, whisking with a fork as you do so. Spoon the mince into the pastry case and cover with the milk mixture – it will seep down a bit. Return the pie to the oven and cook for another 30 minutes. After this time, sprinkle with cheese and cook for another 15–20 minutes, or until a rich golden brown. Loosen the pie carefully with a palette knife and serve.

INDIAN MEATBALLS
· STUFFED WITH CHEESE ·

- 500g lean beef or lamb mince
- 8 cardamom pods
- 2 tsp coriander seeds
- 6–8 whole cloves
- 3–4 large garlic cloves, finely chopped
- sea salt
- 3–4 pinches of chilli powder
- 1 large egg, lightly whisked
- 1 tbsp groundnut or sunflower oil, plus extra for oiling
- 100g soft white cheese
- plain flour, for dusting
- a good handful of coriander leaves, roughly chopped

SERVES 4–5

I love eating things with hidden surprises, and meatballs provide a perfect opportunity. Here the soft cheese centre blends perfectly with the spiced meat; lovely for a summer meal served with mint leaves and a crunchy onion salad.

Place the minced beef in a large mixing bowl and mash thoroughly using a wooden spoon until pasty and sticky. Carefully make a small incision in the cardamom pods and extract all the seeds. Place the cardamom seeds, coriander seeds and cloves into a coffee grinder or pestle and mortar and grind to a fine powder. Using a pestle and mortar or a small bowl and metal spoon, pound and grind the garlic with a teaspoon of sea salt until you have a purée. Stir the freshly ground spices, garlic purée, chilli powder and egg into the meat until thoroughly combined.

Using wet hands, form the mixture into ping-pong sized balls. Oil a flat surface and flatten the balls out into fairly thin circles. Put a teaspoon of the soft cheese into the centre of each meat circle and carefully bring the meat up and around the cheese so that it is completely enclosed. Spread some flour on a board or flat surface and roll the meatballs in the flour until thinly coated.

Heat the oil in a large frying pan over a medium heat. Fry the meatballs for 5–8 minutes, turning carefully until browned all over. Transfer the meatballs to a serving bowl and scatter with the coriander leaves before serving.

· WELLINGTON PIES ·

- 500g lean beef mince
- a bunch of spring onions, trimmed and finely chopped
- 1 rounded tsp green peppercorns, in brine and drained
- sea salt and freshly ground black pepper
- 2 x 85g tins of smoked oysters, drained

For the pastry:
- 4 tbsp olive oil, plus extra for oiling
- 175g strong plain white flour or white spelt flour
- ½ tsp sea salt
- 2 tbsp water

SERVES 8

These little open-topped pies can be served at room temperature as part of a light lunch or at a supper party. The lean beef is still pink in the centre and holds a layer of smoked oysters, which imparts a lovely smoky flavour to the whole pie. The crisp pastry is similar to a good hot water crust on a pork pie but is instead made with olive oil.

Oil 8 deep patty or muffin tins. To make the pastry, sift the flour and the salt into a mixing bowl. Heat the olive oil with the water and as soon as it begins to bubble remove from the heat. Gradually pour the hot liquid into the flour, stirring with a wooden spoon as you do so. Divide the warm dough into 8 pieces and using your fingers press each piece into a tin to line it, bringing the dough about 1–1½cm above the top edge. Place the tins in the fridge for 30 minutes.

Preheat the oven to 200°C/Gas mark 6. Place the dough-lined tins in the centre of the oven and bake blind for 15 minutes, or until golden brown. Meanwhile, in a large bowl, mix the beef, spring onions, peppercorns and seasoning until well combined.

Once the pastry is cooked, put a heaped teaspoon of the beef mixture into each tin. Lay the smoked oysters on top, dividing them equally between the tins. Spoon the remaining beef mixture on top, heaping the meat so that the oysters are completely covered.

Turn the oven up to 230°C/Gas mark 8. Return the tins to the oven and cook for 10–15 minutes, or until the meat is just browned on top.

BEEF & COCONUT
· CURRY ·

For 25 years I lived beside a London common; every May, when the chestnut trees became covered in flowering candles, we knew the fair was about to arrive. It stayed for two weeks and my children begged to go almost every day. Someone in our family would invariably win a coconut and this mild curry originated with one of these. I would throw the coconut onto the stone-tiled floor of my kitchen to break it and then extract the flesh laboriously, grinding and pressing it through a sieve to make coconut milk. Thankfully tinned coconut milk has replaced this complicated process. Serve with some basmati rice.

Cut the chillies open under running water, discard the seeds and chop the flesh finely. Melt the butter with the oil in a flameproof casserole dish over a medium heat. Add the garlic, ginger, onion, ground coriander and cardamom and stir for a minute. Turn up the heat and add the beef. Stir with a wooden spoon until the meat has separated and browned, about 5–8 minutes, then turn the heat down. Mix the tomato purée with the water and stir into the meat mixture. Add the chopped tomatoes and cover. Leave to simmer very gently, stirring occasionally, for about 20 minutes.

Stir in the okra and season with salt. Re-cover the dish and leave to simmer for another 5–8 minutes. Just before serving pour in the coconut milk and only roughly combine. Sprinkle with the coriander leaves and serve.

- 2 green chillies
- 25g butter
- 1 tbsp groundnut oil
- 3 large garlic cloves, finely chopped
- 5–8cm piece of ginger, peeled and finely chopped
- 1 red onion, finely chopped
- 2 tsp ground coriander seeds
- 1 tsp ground cardamom seeds
- 500g beef mince
- 1 tbsp tomato purée
- 2 tbsp water
- 400g chopped tomatoes
- 225g fresh okra, trimmed
- sea salt
- 400ml coconut milk
- a handful of coriander, roughly chopped

SERVES 6

STUFFED PEPPERS
· GRATINÉE ·

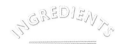

- 25g butter, plus extra for baking
- 1 heaped tbsp plain flour
- 150ml whole milk
- 100g strong Cheddar, coarsely grated
- 25g Parmesan, freshly grated, plus extra for baking
- sea salt and freshly ground black pepper
- 350g beef mince
- 50g fresh breadcrumbs
- 2–3 large garlic cloves, finely chopped
- 8–10 sage leaves, finely chopped
- 2 tbsp tomato purée
- 1 tsp paprika
- 3 large, fresh plum tomatoes
- 1 large onion, thinly sliced
- 1 rounded tsp caster sugar
- 3 peppers, halved and seeds and stems removed

SERVES 4–6

During the 1960s and '70s there was a craze for stuffed peppers. As many were fairly dull I devised this variation. These 'pepper boats' (so named by my children) are a great favourite in my family and are very good served with new potatoes and green beans.

Melt the butter in a saucepan, remove from the heat and stir in the flour. Blend to a paste and gradually add in the milk. Return to the heat and bring to the boil, stirring all the time. Let the sauce bubble, still stirring, for 2–3 minutes, or until very thick. Mix in the Cheddar and remove from the heat. Thoroughly mix until the cheese has melted and you have a smooth sauce. Add the Parmesan and season to taste. Set aside to cool.

In a bowl, mix the mince with the breadcrumbs, garlic, sage, tomato purée and paprika. Season well. Make a small incision in the tomatoes and cover with boiling water. Leave for a minute or two, then drain. Remove and discard the tomato skin and finely chop the flesh. Spread the tomato and onion out on the bottom of a large ovenproof dish, season and sprinkle with sugar.

Bring a pan of salted water to the boil, reduce the heat and simmer the peppers for 6–8 minutes until soft. Drain the peppers and fill each with the meat mixture. Preheat the oven to 180°C/Gas mark 4.

Lay the stuffed peppers on the onion and tomato mixture. Cover with the cheese sauce, sprinkle with the extra Parmesan and dot with more butter. Cook uncovered in the centre of the oven for 50–60 minutes, or until the tops have browned.

MEATLOAF
· WITH BLUE CHEESE ·

- butter, for greasing
- 500g beef mince
- 75g chestnut mushrooms, finely chopped
- 100g smoked rindless streaky bacon, finely chopped
- 1 large garlic clove, finely chopped
- 1 small onion, finely chopped
- 50g fresh brown breadcrumbs
- 1 rounded tsp dried oregano
- 6 tbsp tomato ketchup
- 2 eggs, lightly whisked
- sea salt and freshly ground black pepper
- 100g Saint Agur or Gorgonzola cheese
- 1 tbsp whole milk
- ½ tsp mild chilli powder

SERVES 4–5

I never tire of this. After I tasted American meatloaf in New York in 1967 I began experimenting with different versions; this is the one I, and all others who have tried it, like best. Baked potatoes or perhaps even more suitable, baked sweet potatoes, can be cooked in the oven at the same time, but I prefer it served with a crisp green salad.

Preheat the oven to 180°C/Gas mark 4 and butter a 1kg loaf tin. In a large bowl, mix the beef, mushrooms, bacon, garlic and onion. Once combined, add the breadcrumbs, oregano, 3 tablespoons of the tomato ketchup and half the egg. Stir the mixture until thoroughly mixed and season generously with salt and pepper.

Spoon half the mixture into the loaf tin and spread level. Crumble the cheese into a small bowl and stir in the milk, remaining egg and chilli powder. Pour the cheese mixture over the mince. Spoon the remaining mince into the tin and spread level. Cook the loaf in the centre of the oven for 1 hour, or until browned, then remove and set aside to cool slightly.

Turn up the oven to 240°C/Gas mark 9. Loosen the sides of the loaf with a knife and turn out carefully into a shallow ovenproof dish. Smear the top of the loaf with the remaining tomato ketchup and put back in the hot oven. Cook for 10–15 minutes, or until the tomato glaze is lightly speckled black. Before serving leave the meatloaf to stand at room temperature for 8–10 minutes. Cut into thick slices and serve.

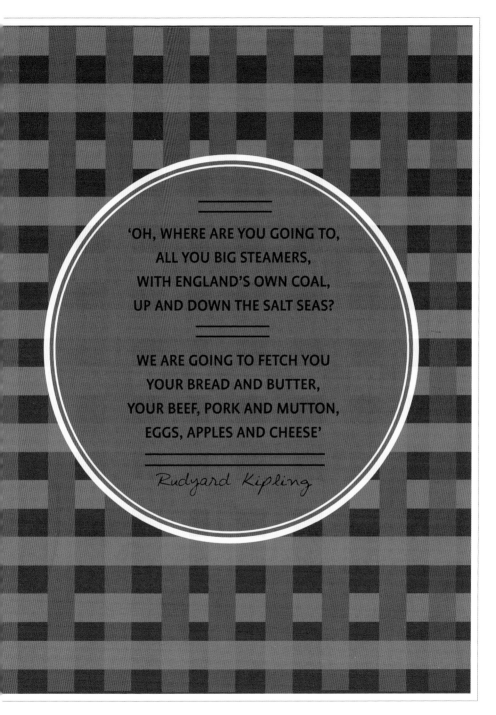

'OH, WHERE ARE YOU GOING TO,
ALL YOU BIG STEAMERS,
WITH ENGLAND'S OWN COAL,
UP AND DOWN THE SALT SEAS?

WE ARE GOING TO FETCH YOU
YOUR BREAD AND BUTTER,
YOUR BEEF, PORK AND MUTTON,
EGGS, APPLES AND CHEESE'

Rudyard Kipling

OLD ENGLISH
• LATTICE FLAN •

- 450g potatoes, peeled
- sea salt and freshly ground black pepper
- 75g butter, cut into cubes
- 175g strong white plain flour or white spelt flour
- 500g beef mince
- 4 tsp horseradish sauce
- 1 onion, finely chopped
- 2 tbsp tomato purée
- 50g raisins
- ¼ whole nutmeg, freshly grated
- 50g tinned anchovy fillets, oil reserved

SERVES 6

I conceived this dish after reading a book about early English food and it incorporates flavour combinations typical of the seventeenth century. Usually pastry dishes are best eaten hot or at least warm, but this is just as good cold, making it perfect for a picnic or cold buffet.

Boil the potatoes in salted water until they yield and feel soft when pierced with a small knife or skewer, then drain and mash until smooth. Season and mix in the butter. Sift in the flour and stir together thoroughly. Gather up the lump of dough and press over the bottom and up the sides of a 23cm earthenware flan dish.

Place the mince in a bowl with the horseradish sauce, onion, tomato purée, raisins and grated nutmeg. Season well and stir until combined.

Preheat the oven to 200°C/Gas mark 6. Spoon the beef mixture into the dough-lined flan dish and spread level. Arrange the anchovy fillets in a criss-cross pattern on top of the meat and pour the reserved anchovy oil over the top. Cook on the centre shelf of the oven for 25–30 minutes, or until browned.

· FARMHOUSE PIE ·

INGREDIENTS

- 500g beef or lamb mince
- 1 heaped tsp paprika
- sea salt and freshly ground black pepper
- 2 tbsp sunflower oil
- 2 tbsp tomato purée
- 50g butter
- 50g plain flour
- 450ml milk
- 100g strong Cheddar or other hard cheese, grated
- 2 large onions, sliced into thin rings

SERVES 5–6

Ignoring the grey watery mince of my schooldays, I created this sophisticated version of a Shepherd's pie by adding spices I remembered from my time spent in Syria. I have never wavered in my love of this infinitely adaptable and comforting dish. Both adults and children love it (even when you add flavours they would normally scorn) and this version has a lovely cheese and onion topping.

Season the mince with the paprika, salt and pepper. Heat 1 tablespoon of the sunflower oil in a large frying pan, add the mince and fry over a fairly high heat until the mince has separated and browned all over. Stir in the tomato purée and transfer the meat to an ovenproof dish. Set aside the frying pan for later.

Meanwhile, make the topping. Melt the butter in a saucepan, remove from the heat and stir in the flour until a smooth paste has formed. Gradually stir in the milk and put back on the heat. Bring to the boil. Allow to bubble gently, stirring all the time, for 2–3 minutes, or until thick and smooth. Stir in the grated cheese until melted. Remove from the heat and season to taste.

Preheat the oven to 200°C/Gas mark 6. In the reserved frying pan, heat the remaining oil and fry the onions over a fairly high heat until softened and golden brown. Stir the onions into the cheese sauce and spoon the topping over the mince. Bake in the top of the oven for 20–30 minutes, or until a rich golden brown.

CHILLI CON
· CARNE EXTRA ·

- 2 tbsp olive oil
- 2 onions, sliced into rings
- 500g lean beef mince
- 2 tsp ground cinnamon
- 1–3 small red or green chillies
- 2 x 400g tins of red kidney beans
- 400g tin of chopped tomatoes
- sea salt
- 25g dark chocolate, at least 70% cocoa solids
- 2 tbsp water
- a handful of flat-leaf parsley, roughly chopped

SERVES 6

In Mexico, Spain and Italy a small amount of dark chocolate – which we are now told is good for us – is used to add richness and texture to savoury dishes. It is especially good in spicy dishes, as I found when I made a quick version of this old favourite. Using fresh chillies instead of powder is also a plus; one small green chilli will make a fairly mild version which most children will eat, but if you prefer a real kick increase the number of chillies accordingly.

Heat the olive oil in a large, heavy-based casserole dish over a medium heat. Add the onions and stir around for 1–2 minutes until softened and lightly browned. Increase the heat, add the beef mince and stir for 2–3 minutes, or until separated and browned. Mix in the cinnamon and remove from the heat.

Cut the chillies open lengthways under running water, remove the stem and seeds and thinly slice the flesh. Drain the kidney beans and add them to the casserole dish together with the sliced chillies. Stir through the chopped tomatoes and season generously with salt.

Break the chocolate into a small saucepan and add the water. Place over a very low heat and stir until the chocolate has melted into the water, then add to the meat mixture. Cover the casserole dish and return to the heat. Bring to a bubbling point, then turn down the heat and leave to simmer gently for 10–15 minutes. Just before serving stir in the parsley.

· KATE'S PIE ·

INGREDIENTS

- 4 whole eggs
- olive oil, for frying
- 2 large garlic cloves, finely chopped
- ½–1 tsp mild chilli powder
- 500g lean beef mince
- 1 tbsp tomato purée
- sea salt
- 175g frozen sweetcorn
- 50g butter
- 25g plain flour, plus extra for dusting
- 600ml milk, plus extra for glazing
- a large handful of flat-leaf parsley, chopped
- 250g puff pastry

SERVES 6

From the age of three my youngest daughter Kate liked pies above all else. 'I just want a pie' she used to wail with the powerful voice that has turned her into the singer she is today. So I made this; I knew she would love it as it included two of her favourite things, beef and sweetcorn. The 'grown-ups' wolfed it down too.

In a saucepan of cold water, bring the eggs to a gentle boil, reduce the heat and simmer for 7 minutes. Dip in cold water, peel, roughly chop and set aside. Heat a little oil in a frying pan over a medium heat. Add the garlic and chilli, mix briefly, then add the beef. Stir with a wooden spoon until the beef has separated and browned, and any liquid has evaporated. Mix in the tomato purée and a little salt and remove from the heat. Add the sweetcorn and eggs and turn into a shallow, 1.7-litre ovenproof dish.

Melt the butter in a saucepan, remove from the heat and mix in the flour to create a paste. Gradually stir in the milk and place back on the heat. Bring the mixture to the boil, stirring constantly, and then let bubble, while stirring, for 2–3 minutes. Remove from the heat and add the parsley. Pour over the mince mixture and leave to cool.

Preheat the oven to 220°C/Gas mark 7. On a lightly floured surface, roll out the pastry until slightly bigger than the pie dish. Cut off a thin strip all the way around the edge of the rolled pastry, moisten with water and press around the edges of the ovenproof dish. Wet this strip of pastry and lightly press the rolled pastry on top of the pie to seal. Trim and use any scraps to decorate the top of the pie. Pierce two holes in the centre and brush with a little milk. Bake in the oven for 20–25 minutes, or until the pastry is a rich golden brown.

CURRIED BEEF
• SURPRISE CAKE •

- 4 large eggs
- 500g lean beef mince
- 3 rounded tsp tikka masala paste
- 2 large garlic cloves, very finely chopped
- a handful of mint or coriander leaves, chopped
- sea salt
- olive oil, for brushing

SERVES 6–8

I remember the excitement I felt when I first made this as an easy supper; I thought it was a slightly mad experiment and when it worked I couldn't believe that anything as easy could be so magical. The real surprise is that the poached eggs buried within magically retain their soft centres – as you cut into the centre of the juicy, spicy beef cake you release a running softness of bright orange egg yolk.

Poach the eggs lightly until the whites are just set, about 6 minutes. Immediately plunge them into cold water to prevent any further cooking.

Place the beef in a mixing bowl and mix in the curry paste, garlic, mint and some salt. Spread half the mixture into a 15cm cake tin – not one with a loose base – pressing it level with a wooden spoon. Then make four equally spaced depressions with a large metal spoon and place a poached egg into each. Cover with the remaining beef and pat level. Brush the top with a little oil.

Preheat the oven to 240°C/Gas mark 9. Place the beef cake on a high shelf in the oven for 15–20 minutes, or until a darkish brown. Do not cook for any longer than 20 minutes, otherwise the egg will no longer be runny. Remove from the oven and carefully pour the juices out of the tin into a small saucepan. Boil the juices fiercely over a high heat for 2–4 minutes until reduced and syrupy. Carefully turn the cake out of the tin and place onto a serving plate. Spoon the reduced juices over the cake to glaze and serve immediately, cut into slices like a conventional cake.

LITTLE MEATBALLS IN A GOAT'S
• CHEESE SAUCE •

INGREDIENTS

- 350g beef mince
- 100g semolina
- 2 rounded tbsp tomato purée
- 3 large garlic cloves, finely chopped
- 2 tsp dried oregano
- sea salt and freshly ground black pepper
- 1 tbsp olive or sunflower oil

For the sauce:
- 25g butter
- 2 rounded tbsp plain flour
- 600ml milk
- 225g hard mature goat's cheese, grated
- 150ml soured cream or crème fraîche
- ¼–½ whole nutmeg, freshly grated
- sea salt and freshly ground black pepper
- Parmesan, freshly grated, to serve

SERVES 5–6

I suppose you could say that these meatballs, with their tomato, garlic and oregano flavouring, have a slightly Greek or Italian character. Whatever the case they are another family and entertainment-friendly dish that can be made ahead and kept warm, giving out a smell that would make even vegetarians salivate. The mingling flavours and textures go really well with broad beans or lightly cooked cauliflower.

To make the meatballs, put the mince in a bowl and add the semolina, tomato purée, garlic and oregano. Season generously and mix thoroughly with a wooden spoon. Wet your hands and form the mixture into small balls, about the size of a largish marble. Preheat the oven to 180°C/Gas mark 4.

Heat the oil in a large frying pan and fry the meatballs over a fairly high heat, turning them continuously for 5–8 minutes, or until dark brown all over. Using a slotted spoon, transfer the meatballs to a shallow ovenproof dish; they should fairly loosely cover the bottom.

To make the sauce, melt the butter in a heavy-based saucepan. Remove from the heat, stir in the flour with a wooden spoon and then gradually stir in the milk. Put back on the heat and bring to the boil, stirring constantly and allowing it to bubble for about 3 minutes. Mix in the goat's cheese. Once it has melted, mix in the soured cream, nutmeg and some seasoning.

Pour the sauce over the meatballs so that they are covered. Sprinkle with Parmesan and cook in the centre of the oven for 30–40 minutes, or until browned.

PENNE WITH BEEF, SMOKED OYSTERS AND BABY SPINACH

- 8 whole cloves
- 1 tsp coriander seeds
- 300g lean beef mince
- sea salt and freshly ground black pepper
- 2 tbsp groundnut oil
- 3 large garlic cloves, finely chopped
- 2 x 85g tins of smoked oysters
- 250–300g dried penne
- 2 tbsp extra virgin olive oil
- 250–300g baby spinach leaves
- shavings of Parmesan, to serve

SERVES 4

When I was writing a biographical family story that had nothing to do with food I had almost no time for cooking. I used to shop first thing and then work until evening when I would rush downstairs to cook supper as fast as I could. So it was often pasta. This is one of those quick suppers: the smoked oysters – or you can use smoked mussels – give the dish an enhanced flavour. A wok is better than a frying pan for this.

Using a pestle and mortar or an electric coffee grinder, grind the cloves and coriander seeds to a powder. Put the mince in a mixing bowl and stir through the ground spices and some seasoning. Heat the groundnut oil in a wok over a high heat and add the mince. Cook, while stirring, until the meat has separated and browned, about 6–10 minutes. Mix in the garlic and stir for another minute. Remove the wok from the heat and add the smoked oysters and their oil.

Bring a saucepan of salted water to the boil, drop in the penne and cook until just tender, about 8–10 minutes. Drain and transfer to a heated bowl, stirring in the olive oil as you do so. Put the wok containing the mince back on to the heat, add the spinach leaves and cook for barely a minute, just until the leaves go limp. Tip the mixture into the bowl of penne, roughly combine and serve at once with some Parmesan.

THE COMPLETE
· PICNIC LOAF ·

INGREDIENTS

- 1 small wholemeal or multigrain loaf
- butter, for frying and greasing
- 250g leeks, trimmed
- 250g beef mince
- 2 tbsp tomato purée
- 50g strong Cheddar cheese, grated
- 2 large garlic cloves, finely chopped
- 2 rounded tsp ground coriander
- sea salt and freshly ground black pepper
- 1 large egg, lightly whisked

SERVES 6

I first had this idea for our frequent picnics in south Devon during my children's school holidays; it is tasty, convenient and sustaining since meat, vegetables and cheese are cooked together within a bread crust. To keep the loaf warm on the journey I keep it wrapped in the cooking foil and enclosed in an insulated bag, but it also tastes good cold.

Using a sharp bread knife, slice off one end of the loaf. Carefully pull out all of the insides and place the empty loaf and the cut end to one side. Blitz the insides in a food processor to make breadcrumbs. Over a medium heat, add a generous knob of butter to a large frying pan and fry the crumbs, stirring constantly until browned and crisp.

Chop the leeks finely and put into a large bowl. Mix in the beef mince, the tomato purée, cheese, garlic and ground coriander. Season well and mix in the fried breadcrumbs and the egg until well combined.

Preheat the oven to 190°C/Gas mark 5. Spoon the leek and beef mixture into the empty loaf crust, pressing it in slightly and filling it right to the brim. Replace the end of the loaf to enclose the meat mixture and secure it with a long skewer. Smear the loaf all over with butter – be especially generous on top – and wrap in foil.

Put the foil package in a roasting tray and cook just below the centre of the oven for 1 hour. Take a chopping board and sharp knife with you to the picnic and cut the loaf into fairly thick slices just before serving.

BEEF AND ANCHOVY
• MEATBALLS •

- 75g white or brown bread with crusts removed
- milk, for soaking
- 400g lean beef mince
- 50g tinned anchovy fillets, oil reserved
- 2–3 large garlic cloves, finely chopped
- a handful of flat-leaf parsley or sage leaves, finely chopped, plus extra to serve
- sea salt and freshly ground black pepper
- plain flour, for dusting
- 1 tbsp olive oil
- butter, for frying
- 150ml soured cream

SERVES 4–5

These simple meatballs include milk soaked bread which makes them soft and juicy as it prevents any liquid from running off as the meatballs cook. You can use yogurt instead of soured cream if you prefer.

Roughly tear the bread into pieces and place in a mixing bowl. Pour over enough milk to cover and mash with a fork until pasty. Stir in the mince, the oil from the anchovies and the garlic. Mix together using a wooden spoon. Finely chop the anchovy fillets and add them to the mince mixture along with the parsley, a little salt and plenty of pepper. Wet your hands to prevent the mixture from sticking and form the mince into walnut-sized balls. Place the meatballs onto a lightly floured board or flat surface and roll to lightly coat in flour.

Heat the olive oil and butter in a large frying pan over a medium heat and fry the meatballs for about 6–8 minutes, turning them frequently until a rich golden brown all over. Transfer the meatballs to a warmed serving dish using a slotted spoon. Pour over the soured cream and sprinkle with a few leaves of parsley to serve.

SURPRISE
· AVOCADOS ·

INGREDIENTS

- 3 ripe avocados
- 1 large lemon, plus the juice of 1 lemon
- 1 tbsp red wine vinegar
- 2 egg yolks
- 2 rounded tsp wholegrain mustard
- a handful of flat-leaf parsley, finely chopped
- 2–3 tarragon sprigs, finely chopped
- 1 tbsp extra virgin olive oil, plus extra to serve
- 350g extra lean freshly minced beef
- sea salt and freshly ground black pepper

SERVES 6

This first course really is a surprise, and a very popular one. Under a deceptive topping of lemon slices is a sensual filling of tender raw beef mixed with avocado, egg yolks, herbs and mustard. Only ever use very fresh, and never frozen, beef for this dish.

Using a sharp knife, cut the avocados in half lengthways and carefully remove the stone. Cut a very thin slice off the top of each avocado half, including the skin. Smear these slices with a little of the lemon juice to prevent discolouration and leave to one side.

Spoon the remaining avocado flesh out of the shells and into a bowl. Do not throw away the shells. Add the remaining lemon juice and the vinegar to the avocado flesh and mash well with a fork. Stir the egg yolks in thoroughly, followed by the mustard, herbs and the olive oil. Once mixed, add in the beef mince and seasoning.

Fill the empty avocado shells with the mince mixture and make level. Lay the reserved avocado slices back on top of each of the filled shells and place the avocados onto individual plates. Using a small, sharp knife, carefully halve the lemon lengthways and very thinly slice. Arrange the semicircles of lemon so that they cover the centre of each avocado half. You should not be able to see the mince filling. Before serving drizzle over a little olive oil.

SPINACH AND BEEF
· LAYER PIE ·

- sea salt and freshly ground black pepper
- 500g large leaf spinach, stalks removed
- 25g butter, plus extra for greasing
- 500g beef mince
- 2 rounded tsp paprika
- 2 tbsp plain flour
- 600ml tomato juice
- finely grated zest and juice of ½ an orange
- 2–4 pinches of mild chilli powder
- 2 large eggs
- 75g blanched almonds, chopped

SERVES 6–8

When I was living with my grandmother as a child the doctor told her I was anaemic so she gave me lots of spinach and watercress. Thankfully I wasn't put off and to this day spinach is one of my favourite vegetables. I was gratified when I dreamt up this pie; it has a wonderful crunchy top and is undeniably healthy.

Bring a large pan of salted water to the boil. Plunge in the spinach leaves and boil for about 30 seconds, just until the leaves are limp. Drain well, pressing with a wooden spoon to extract all the liquid.

Melt the butter in a heavy saucepan. Add the mince and stir over a high heat until the beef has separated and browned. Remove from the heat and stir in the paprika and flour. Gradually mix in the tomato juice and return to the heat. While stirring, bring to the boil and cook for 3 minutes, or until thickened. Stir in the orange zest and juice, chilli powder and season with salt.

Preheat the oven to 200°C/Gas mark 6 and butter a 1–1.5 litre ovenproof dish. Spread a thin layer of the meat mixture on the bottom of the dish and cover with a thin layer of spinach. Repeat the layering with the rest of the mixtures, ending with spinach.

Whisk the eggs in a bowl, season with salt and pepper and stir in the almonds. Cover the spinach with the egg mixture and cook in the centre of the oven for 25 minutes.

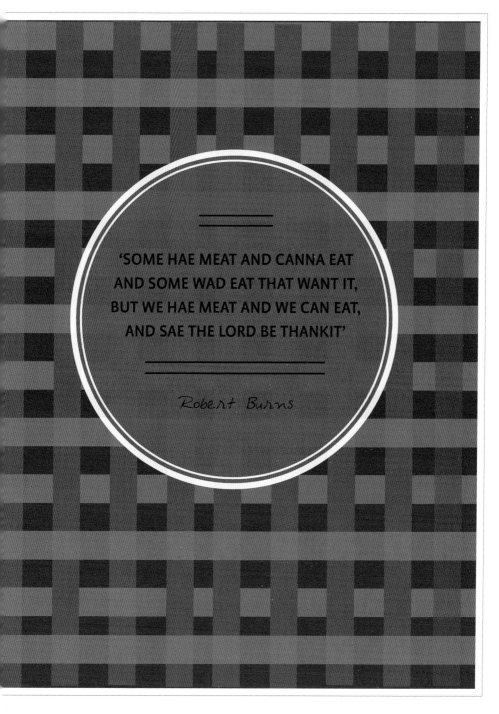

'SOME HAE MEAT AND CANNA EAT
AND SOME WAD EAT THAT WANT IT,
BUT WE HAE MEAT AND WE CAN EAT,
AND SAE THE LORD BE THANKIT'

Robert Burns

CHUTNEY STUFFED
• MEATBALLS •

- 100g bulgur wheat
- 500g beef mince
- 1 large garlic clove, finely chopped
- sea salt and freshly ground black pepper
- 4 tbsp chutney
- a handful of mint and coriander leaves, chopped
- 1 large egg, lightly whisked
- groundnut or sunflower oil, for frying

SERVES 4–5

The first time I made these I stuffed them with mango chutney, but I have also used one of my own chutneys made with tomatoes, sweet peppers and onions; you really can use whatever you like best. The crunchy coating of bulgur wheat combines perfectly with the deliciously soft chutney centre.

Put the bulgur wheat into a bowl, cover with plenty of cold water and leave to soak. Place the beef mince in a mixing bowl and stir in the garlic and seasoning using a wooden spoon. Place the chutney in a separate small bowl and stir through the mint and coriander. Take up enough mince to form into a ping-pong sized ball and then flatten it in the palm of your hand so it looks like a small burger. Put about half a teaspoon of chutney in the centre of the flattened mince and then very gently bring up the sides to enclose the chutney completely. Lightly pat it into a ball shape again. Repeat with the rest of the mince and chutney.

Drain the bulgur wheat in a sieve and press out the moisture using a wooden spoon. Transfer to a small bowl. Place the egg in another small bowl and, one at a time, dip the meatballs into the egg and then into the bulgur, lightly patting it on to coat thickly.

Pour groundnut oil into a large, deep frying pan to a depth of about 4cm. Put the pan over a very high heat and when it is really hot carefully add the meatballs; you may need to do this in batches. Fry, turning carefully once, for about 2–3 minutes on each side until light golden brown. Lift the meatballs out with a slotted spoon and drain on absorbent kitchen paper. Eat as soon as possible.

• FAR EASTERN PIE •

- 500g spinach, stalks removed
- sea salt
- 50g butter
- 2 rounded tsp ground coriander seeds
- 1 rounded tsp ground cinnamon
- 1 tsp ground turmeric
- 4 large garlic cloves, finely chopped
- 3cm piece of ginger, peeled and finely chopped
- 700g beef mince
- juice of ½ lemon
- 2 tbsp desiccated coconut
- 40g ground rice
- 400ml coconut milk
- 500ml whole milk
- 2–3 pinches of hot chilli powder

SERVES 6–7

When I first made this pie you could not buy tinned coconut milk so I had to invent a laborious method of boiling fresh coconut in milk. Thankfully there is no need for that now! If possible always use whole spices and grind them yourself – they are far more aromatic.

Plunge the spinach into a saucepan of boiling salted water for a minute, or until the leaves go limp. Drain and press out any liquid. Roughly chop the leaves.

Heat 25g of the butter in a large frying pan over a medium heat. Add the coriander, cinnamon and turmeric and cook for no more than half a minute to release the aromas. Stir in the garlic and ginger and cook for another 30 seconds. Mix in the mince, increase the heat and dig at it with a wooden spoon to break it up as it cooks – remove from the heat once the mince has browned all over. Stir in the spinach and the lemon juice and spoon into an open, fairly shallow ovenproof dish. Set to one side.

Preheat the oven to 190°C/Gas mark 5. Place the desiccated coconut in a bowl and cover with boiling water. Leave to one side. In a saucepan, mix together the ground rice, coconut milk and whole milk. While stirring, bring the mixture to the boil. Turn down the heat and allow to simmer gently, for about 5 minutes, or until thick. Season with salt and spoon the sauce over the meat mixture. Sprinkle with the chilli powder.

Drain the desiccated coconut. Melt the remaining butter in a saucepan, remove from the heat and stir in the drained coconut. Spoon over the pie and cook in the oven for 35–45 minutes, or until a rich golden brown.

PORK
&VEAL

MYBUBBLE
•ANDSQUEAK•

INGREDIENTS

- 500g waxy potatoes, such as Charlotte
- 1 tbsp olive oil
- 2 large garlic cloves, finely chopped
- 1 tsp caraway seeds
- 300g lean pork mince
- 200g sweetheart (pointed) cabbage, very thinly sliced
- ¼ whole nutmeg, grated
- sea salt and freshly ground black pepper

SERVES 4–5

I don't actually know why I called this bubble and squeak because apart from including cooked potatoes and cabbage it isn't anything like it. However the addition of well-flavoured pork makes it a quick and healthy all-in-one family dish. I used to use dill seeds as well as the caraway seeds but I have now replaced the dill with nutmeg, which I think tastes even better.

Cut the unpeeled potatoes into small cubes and steam or boil until cooked. Heat the olive oil in a large, deep sauté pan over a medium heat and add the garlic and caraway seeds. Mix for 30 seconds, then add the pork mince and cook for 4–5 minutes, or until the meat has separated and browned.

Stir in the cabbage and cook for 2–3 minutes, or until limp. Add the nutmeg and cooked potato cubes and stir for another minute to reheat them. Season to taste with salt and pepper and serve.

· PIGLET PIE ·

- 1 tbsp sunflower oil
- 350g lean pork mince
- sea salt and freshly ground black pepper
- 2 tsp coriander seeds, ground to a powder
- 2 tsp wholegrain mustard
- 4 fresh plum tomatoes, chopped fairly small
- 225g frozen or tinned sweetcorn

For the pastry:
- 100g plain flour, plus extra for dusting
- 1 tsp baking powder
- sea salt
- 100g cold butter, cut into cubes
- 175g cold mashed potato
- milk, for glazing

SERVES 4–5

Wherever I go, this is one of my recipes which decades later people still remember and tell me about. They talk about how their children adored it, what a perfect family dish it was and how they like the name! This pie has an especially good crust of potato pastry, and is a perfect way to use up any leftover mashed potato. Delicious served with green beans and mangetout.

Heat the oil in a large frying pan over a fairly high heat. Add the mince and some seasoning and, while stirring, cook until separated and lightly browned. Stir in the ground coriander, mustard and tomatoes and cook for another 4–5 minutes. Mix in the sweetcorn and transfer to a 1–1¼ litre capacity pie dish. Set aside to cool.

Meanwhile, make the pastry. Sift the flour, baking powder and a generous pinch of salt into a bowl. Add the butter and, using your hands, rub into the flour until it looks like breadcrumbs. Add the mashed potato and lightly knead until you have a smooth dough. Shape into a ball and roll out on a floured board until a bit larger than the top of the pie dish. Cut a thin strip off the edges of the pastry and press this strip around the rim of the pie dish. Dampen with a little water and lay the large piece of pastry on top. Press down the edges to seal and trim away any excess if necessary. Make small incisions covering the top of the pie – in a pattern if you wish – using the back of a knife. If you have any excess pastry use it to make decorations for the top of the pie; I made a rather strange looking pig!

Preheat the oven to 190°C/Gas mark 5. Brush the pastry with a little milk and cook in the centre of the oven for 25–35 minutes, or until golden brown all over.

RISSOLES WITH A
• FENNEL SURPRISE •

INGREDIENTS

- 2–3 fennel bulbs, about 350–450g, stalks removed and leaves reserved
- olive oil, for oiling
- 675g pork mince
- 100g fresh breadcrumbs
- finely grated zest of 1 orange
- a handful of dill leaves, roughly chopped
- 1 large egg, beaten
- sea salt and freshly ground black pepper

For the sauce:
- 380g carrots, trimmed and peeled
- 450ml chicken stock
- juice of 1 orange
- 2 tbsp crème fraîche
- sea salt and freshly ground black pepper

SERVES 6–8

A dish of subtle flavours, this is excellent with creamy mash and a mixed leaf salad. If you have no homemade chicken stock use a good-quality stock cube.

Slice the fennel bulbs into 1cm strips and steam or boil for 2–3 minutes, or until just tender. Rinse with cold water. Preheat the oven to 180°C/Gas mark 4. Oil a large roasting tray. Place the mince in a mixing bowl with the breadcrumbs, orange zest, dill, egg and seasoning and mix until combined. Divide the fennel strips into 8 equal piles and, using wet hands to prevent the mixture from sticking, split the mince mixture into 8 balls. On a wet board, press one of the balls of meat out flat. Lay one pile of fennel in the centre and bring the mince up and over to encase the fennel completely. Carefully mould into a fairly round shape. Repeat with the remaining meat and fennel. Lay out in the tray and cover with foil. Cook in the oven for 1 hour, removing the foil for the last 20 minutes.

Meanwhile, make the sauce. Take a 25g piece of carrot, cut it into extremely thin strips and set aside. Roughly chop the remaining carrots. Bring the chicken stock to the boil in a saucepan, add the roughly chopped carrots, reduce the heat and simmer until very soft. Stir in the orange juice and blitz in a food processor until very smooth. Transfer back to the saucepan, add the reserved carrot strips and stir in the crème fraîche. Bring to the boil, bubble for a minute or two and add some seasoning.

Transfer the rissoles to a serving dish and pour the pan juices into a saucepan. Boil fiercely for 3–4 minutes, or until reduced to a syrupy glaze. Spoon over the rissoles and serve with carrot sauce and reserved fennel leaves.

PORK <small>AND</small> BEEF
· ENCROÛTE ·

INGREDIENTS

- olive oil, for oiling
- plain flour, for dusting
- 375g packet of puff pastry
- 1 egg yolk
- 2 tbsp crème fraîche

For the pork mixture:
- 400g pork mince
- 225g Gruyère cheese, cubed
- 4–5cm piece of ginger, peeled and finely chopped
- 2–3 garlic cloves, chopped
- 2 sprigs of rosemary, leaves finely chopped
- 1 egg, beaten
- sea salt and freshly ground black pepper

For the beef mixture:
- 225g lean beef mince
- 3 celery sticks, trimmed and finely chopped
- 175g carrots, peeled and coarsely grated
- 2 tbsp tomato purée
- 2 tsp ground cinnamon
- 2–3 garlic cloves, chopped
- 1 egg, beaten
- sea salt and freshly ground black pepper

SERVES 6

As long as you start in advance and make time for the simple stages, this dish is very straightforward. It's an exciting taste sensation, pronounced luscious by all.

In a large bowl, combine the ingredients for the pork mixture. In another bowl, mix together the beef mixture ingredients. Preheat the oven to 190°C/Gas mark 5. Place a roasting pan half-full of water in the oven. Oil a 1kg loaf tin. In the prepared tin, layer the meat; spoon in half the pork mixture and spread level, then repeat with all the beef mixture and finally the remaining pork. Cover with a piece of oiled foil, place in the roasting pan of water and return to the oven. Cook for 1–1¼ hours, or until the meat has shrunk away from the sides of the tin. Carefully pour the cooking juices out into a small saucepan. Leave the meatloaf in the tin and set aside to cool.

Meanwhile, on a lightly floured surface, roll the pastry into a rectangle about 30 x 25cm. Straighten the edges and keep the trimmings for decoration. Increase the heat of the oven to 220°C/Gas mark 7. Take the cold meatloaf out of the tin and place in the middle of the pastry. Wrap the meat like a parcel, making sure the loaf is fully enclosed. Use a little water to moisten the edges of the pastry and press to seal. Place in an oiled roasting tin seam side down. Decorate with any pastry trimmings. Cut two small slits in the centre to allow steam to escape as it cooks. Brush with egg yolk and cook in the oven for 15–25 minutes, or until a rich golden brown.

Spoon off any fat from the reserved meat juices, stir in the crème fraîche and bring to the boil. Bubble for 2 minutes, or until thick. Transfer to a jug and serve.

GREENDRAGON
· WALNUTMEATBALLS ·

- sea salt
- 1 large green pepper, halved and seeds and stem removed
- 500g pork mince
- 2 large garlic cloves, finely chopped
- 4cm piece of ginger, peeled and finely chopped
- 75g walnuts, chopped
- 1 tbsp tomato purée
- 2 tbsp soy sauce
- 3–4 pinches of mild chilli powder
- 1 tbsp golden caster sugar
- 1 tbsp groundnut or sunflower oil

For the sauce:
- 1½ tbsp soy sauce
- 4 tbsp water
- 3 tsp rice vinegar or white wine vinegar
- 1½ tsp golden caster sugar
- 4–5 spring onions, trimmed and finely chopped

SERVES 4

After a talk I gave at a literary festival recently, a woman from the audience showed me (as many have done over the years) a stained first edition of this book and told me that she has found these served in two different Chinese restaurants, purporting to be a classic Chinese dish. This is far from the case; I dreamt up both the recipe and its title in the 1980s! Quick to prepare, they are good for a lunch, served with noodles and a green salad. If you want to turn them into Red Dragon Walnut Meatballs simply use a red pepper instead.

Bring a small pan of salted water to the boil, add the pepper and cover. Reduce the heat and simmer for 6–8 minutes, or until soft. Drain and chop finely. Place the pork mince in a bowl and add the chopped pepper, garlic, ginger, walnuts, tomato purée and soy sauce and mix until combined. Stir through the chilli powder, sugar and a little salt. Using wet hands to prevent the mixture from sticking, form the meat into ping-pong sized balls.

Heat the oil in a large frying pan and fry the meatballs over a medium heat, for about 20 minutes, or until brown all over. Using a slotted spoon transfer the meatballs to a serving dish and keep warm in a very low oven.

To make the sauce, pour the fat out of the used frying pan but leave the meaty juices. Stir in the soy sauce, water, vinegar and sugar and dissolve over a low heat. Bring to the boil and allow to bubble fiercely for a minute or two, or until it is reduced to a thick, dark syrupy sauce. Remove from the heat and stir in the spring onions. Spoon over the meatballs and serve at once.

· ITALIAN MOUSSAKA ·

- 2 large aubergines, about 700–775g, peeled and thinly sliced into rounds
- juice of 1 lemon
- sea salt and freshly ground black pepper
- 500g veal mince
- 2 large garlic cloves, finely chopped
- 1 rounded tbsp finely chopped rosemary
- 3 tbsp olive oil, plus extra for oiling
- 1 tbsp tomato purée
- 1 onion, roughly chopped
- 500–550g fresh plum tomatoes
- 1 rounded tsp caster sugar
- 125–150g mozzarella cheese, thinly sliced
- a handful of basil leaves, roughly torn

SERVES 6

There are certain ingredients which seem to represent the food of a country more than any others. Tomatoes, mozzarella and veal conjure up Italy, aubergines make me think of Turkey and moussaka reminds me of Greece. This dish is a wonderful mix of all three.

Place the aubergine in a colander set over the sink and cover with half the lemon juice and some salt.

In a bowl, mix the mince, garlic, rosemary and seasoning. Heat a tablespoon of oil in a large frying pan over a high heat. Add the veal mixture and stir for 4–5 minutes, or until the meat has separated and browned and any liquid has evaporated. Stir in the tomato purée and the remaining lemon juice. Transfer to a bowl and set aside.

Put another tablespoon of oil into the used frying pan, turn down the heat and fry the onion until soft. Transfer to the bowl of mince. Make a small incision in each tomato. Cover with boiling water and leave for 1–2 minutes. Drain, peel and discard the skin and halve the flesh lengthways.

Preheat the oven to 180°C/Gas mark 4. Thoroughly rinse the aubergine and pat dry with absorbent kitchen paper. Oil a 1.5–1.8 litre ovenproof dish. Cover the bottom of the dish with half the slices of aubergine and some pepper. Spoon in the mince mixture and spread level. Cover with the remaining aubergine slices and more pepper. Top with the tomato halves, cut side down. Brush with oil and sprinkle over the sugar. Cook in the oven for 1½ hours.

Heat the grill. Cover the dish with mozzarella and cook under the grill for 2–3 minutes, or until the cheese melts. Sprinkle with the basil and serve.

STUFFED EGGS WITH
· VEAL AND PEPPERS ·

- 8 large whole eggs
- 2 red chillies
- 250g veal mince
- 3 sprigs of rosemary, leaves finely chopped
- 1 large orange pepper, seeds and stems removed and finely chopped
- 1 rounded tsp paprika
- sea salt
- 16 whole blanched almonds
- olive oil, for roasting

SERVES 4–6

Stuffed eggs could hardly sound more old-fashioned but these, which I thought up at the start of the 1980s, are a bit different. Adapted as the years have passed, they really have continued to give pleasure through the decades. They can be served hot or cold, either for a main course, a first course or a large party. If you serve them hot they are lovely on a bed of steamed spinach, drizzled with a little olive oil.

Boil the eggs until almost hard-boiled, drain and cover with cold water to cool. Slice the chillies open lengthways under cold water, discard the seeds and stem and chop the flesh finely. Place the veal in a mixing bowl with the chillies, rosemary, pepper, paprika and some salt and stir until well combined.

Preheat the oven to 190°C/Gas mark 5. Remove and discard the eggshells and cut the eggs in half lengthways. Carefully turn the egg yolks out of the egg whites and roughly stir the yolks into the meat mixture. Arrange the halved egg whites in an ovenproof dish. Using your hands, stuff and pile the meat mixture among the halved eggs. Press a blanched almond on the top of each and drizzle over a little oil. Cook in the centre of the oven for 20–25 minutes.

APPLE AND SPINACH
• PORK •

- 1 tbsp olive oil
- 50g butter
- 350g lean pork mince
- 1 heaped tsp coriander seeds, ground to a powder
- sea salt and freshly ground black pepper
- 2 sharp apples, peel and core removed and finely sliced
- 1 tsp finely grated orange zest
- 2 tsp runny honey
- 1 tbsp white wine vinegar
- 225g baby spinach leaves
- 150ml soured cream

SERVES 4

Made in minutes, with a mild and intriguing flavour, this is a good dish for dinner after a tiring day. Perfect with baked or mashed sweet potato.

Heat the oil and 25g of the butter in a large sauté pan over a medium heat. Add the pork and stir to separate and seal the meat. Stir in the ground coriander and some seasoning. Mix in the remaining butter, apples, orange zest, honey and vinegar.

Cover the pan and cook gently for 3–4 minutes, or until the apples are tender. Add the spinach leaves, cover until they wilt and then stir into the meat mixture. Season to taste. Remove from the heat, roughly stir in the soured cream and serve straight from the pan.

· STUFFED TOMATOES ·

- 4 extra large tomatoes
- sea salt and freshly ground black pepper
- 2 tbsp olive oil, plus extra for oiling
- 2 large garlic cloves, finely chopped
- 2 rosemary sprigs, stalks discarded and leaves finely chopped
- 1 rounded tsp coriander seeds, ground to a powder
- 2 tsp clear honey
- 1 tbsp pesto
- 250g pork mince
- 50g Gruyère cheese, grated
- 8 basil leaves, roughly chopped

SERVES 6–8

During the 1970s and '80s, many stuffed tomatoes were stodgy and under-seasoned. I created this recipe to show that they can be full of flavour. It is continually hard to find alternative words for 'delicious'; at the start of the 80s I described these tomatoes as luscious, which is better than 'tasty', a word I try to avoid. Why does the dictionary provide us with so few ways to describe one of the most pleasurable sensations in life?

Slice the tops, including any stem, off the tomatoes and set aside. Use a spoon to scoop out the seeds and most of the flesh and set aside. Salt the insides of the empty tomatoes and lay upside down in a colander to drain.

Heat 1 tablespoon of the oil in a frying pan over a high heat. Chop the insides of the tomatoes and add to the pan with the garlic, rosemary and coriander. Bring to the boil and, while stirring, cook for 4–5 minutes, or until reduced to a fairly thick consistency. Stir in the honey, pesto and seasoning. Transfer to a bowl and set aside.

Heat the remaining oil in the used frying pan over a high heat. Add the mince and seasoning. Cook, stirring continuously, for 5–8 minutes, or until the meat has separated and browned all over. Stir into the tomato sauce and add the Gruyère cheese and basil.

Preheat the oven to 180°C/Gas mark 4 and oil a shallow ovenproof dish. Rinse the tomato shells, pat dry with absorbent kitchen paper and place in the ovenproof dish. Fill with the meat mixture and cover with the reserved tomato tops. Brush with oil and cook for 20–30 minutes.

SURPRISE
· BOMBE SURPRISE ·

- 425g tin of pitted black cherries, in juice
- 50g unblanched whole almonds
- 125g Camembert cheese, cut into 8 pieces
- 1kg lean pork mince
- 2 large garlic cloves, finely chopped
- 1 red onion, finely chopped
- 2 tsp caraway seeds
- sea salt and freshly ground black pepper
- 1 large egg, lightly beaten
- olive oil, for oiling
- 40g flaked almonds
- 2 tsp cornflour
- juice of ½ lemon

SERVES 6–7

Who would think of a bombe surprise made of meat? Oddly enough I did, and it showed me once more how humble mince inspires culinary invention. Here, in the same way as an ice cream bombe, the outer layer hides a mystery interior. It is certainly a conversation piece. You could try using goat's cheese instead of Camembert and walnut halves instead of the almonds.

Strain the cherry juice into a saucepan and set aside. Place the cherries in a bowl and add the whole almonds and Camembert pieces. Put the pork into another bowl and add the garlic, onion and caraway seeds. Season well, add the egg and stir using a wooden spoon.

Preheat the oven to 180°C/Gas mark 4 and lightly oil a roasting pan. Gather up the mince and pat into a large ball. Place in the oiled pan, carefully slice off the top and set to one side. Hollow out the middle of the ball using your hands, bringing the sides up to form a bowl shape. Fill with the cherry mixture. Lightly flatten the reserved meat and lay it on top of the meat bowl, pressing down gently to join it to the sides. Pat to make round. Lightly press the flaked almonds all over the meat.

Cook in the oven for 1¼–1½ hours. Using a wide spatula, transfer the bombe to a warmed serving dish. Pour the pan juices into the saucepan of cherry juice. In a small bowl, mix the cornflour and lemon juice into a paste, then add to the cherry and meat juices. Bring to the boil, then reduce the heat. Simmer gently, while stirring, for 2–3 minutes, or until thickened. Slice the bombe and serve with the sauce.

ROASTPORKSTUFFED
·ᴡɪᴛʜAPRICOTS·

- 25g butter
- 675g fresh apricots, stones removed and roughly chopped
- 2 large garlic cloves
- 2 tsp caster sugar
- 2 tbsp olive oil, plus extra for oiling
- 180g lean pork mince
- 2 tbsp chopped marjoram or 1 tbsp dried oregano
- 3 tsp coriander seeds, ground to a powder
- sea salt and freshly ground black pepper
- plain flour, for dusting
- 1 large red onion, roughly chopped
- 240ml water
- juice of ½ lemon
- 150ml double cream
- 70g wild rocket or other salad leaves

SERVES 6–8

In northern climates apricots are often picked too soon, making them tasteless – but don't give up – an intensity of flavour is magically achieved by cooking, making them delicious in savoury dishes as well as sweet.

Heat the butter in a frying pan over a medium heat, add half the apricots and the garlic and, while stirring, cook for about 5 minutes, or until the apricots are soft and mushy. Stir in the sugar, turn out onto a plate and leave to cool.

Preheat the oven to 180°C/Gas mark 4 and oil a roasting pan. Place the pork in a bowl, add the marjoram, ground coriander and seasoning. Using wet hands, divide the mixture into 4 balls and, on an oiled surface, pat out into large flat burgers. Divide the apricot mixture into 4 and spoon onto the centre of each burger. Carefully draw up the sides of the meat to enclose the apricots and pat into a ball shape. Roll in flour and place in the roasting pan.

Roast in the oven for ¾–1 hour, or until lightly browned. Meanwhile, heat the olive oil in a saucepan over a gentle heat, add the onion and cook until softened. Add the water, the remaining apricots and the lemon juice. Cover and cook over a low heat for 30 minutes, or until very mushy. Remove from the heat and set aside.

Once the balls are cooked, transfer to a warmed plate using a slotted spoon. Pour the pan juices into the saucepan containing the apricot mixture and add the cream and seasoning. Bring to the boil and cook for 1–2 minutes, or until thickened. Place the rocket in a serving dish, pour over the sauce and serve the pork balls on top.

VEAL AND TUNA CROQUETTES
· WITH A CAPER SAUCE ·

- 350g lean veal mince
- 200g tinned tuna in olive oil
- 2 large garlic cloves, crushed
- a large rosemary sprig, finely chopped
- sea salt and freshly ground black pepper
- 1 large egg, beaten
- 1 rounded tsp green peppercorns, in brine
- 25g butter
- 300ml crème fraîche
- 2 rounded tsp capers, roughly crushed
- a small handful of flat-leaf parsley, roughly chopped

SERVES 4

Inspired by the cold Italian dish 'Vitello Tonnato', these croquettes are in fact hot, easy to make and have the same surprisingly delicious marriage of flavours.

Place the veal, the tuna and its oil, the garlic, rosemary and seasoning into a large bowl. Mix together using a wooden spoon until mashed and almost pasty. Stir in the egg and peppercorns. Using wet hands, form the mixture into short sausage shapes.

Melt the butter in a frying pan. Cook the croquettes over a medium heat for 5 minutes on each side, or until golden brown all over. Use a slotted spatula to remove them from the pan and place in a warmed serving dish.

Discard any cooking juices that are in the used frying pan and add the crème fraîche to the pan. Heat until it just begins to bubble, then stir in the capers. Cook for 30 seconds, remove from the heat and season. Pour over the croquettes, sprinkle with parsley and serve.

VEAL AND FENNEL CROQUETTES WITH A WHOLE ROAST CHICKEN

- 250g veal mince
- 1 large fennel bulb
- 1 red pepper, seeds and stem removed and finely chopped
- 2 large garlic cloves, finely chopped
- 2 tsp paprika
- 25g ground rice or fine semolina
- sea salt and freshly ground black pepper
- 3–4 pinches of mild chilli powder
- olive oil, for oiling
- ½ a lemon, cut in half
- 1.5kg free-range chicken
- 250ml crème fraîche or double cream

SERVES 6

The croquettes are cooked with the bird so that the juices mingle in the roasting pan and create a supremely delicious sauce. The only word for this combination is 'yummy'.

Place the veal in a bowl. Cut off the feathery parts of the fennel, chop finely and set aside. Remove and discard any damaged outer parts and the top stems. Finely chop the bulb and add to the mince with the pepper, garlic, paprika and ground rice. Season with salt and chilli powder. Mix together using a wooden spoon. Using oiled hands, form the mixture into ping-pong sized balls.

Preheat the oven to 200°C/Gas mark 6. Place the lemon in the body cavity of the chicken. Smear the skin with a little oil and season with some salt and pepper. Transfer to a large roasting pan and place on the centre shelf of the oven. After 20 minutes of cooking, place the croquettes around the chicken. Return to the oven for 1 hour, or until the chicken is thoroughly cooked – the juices should run clear when the thickest part of the chicken is pierced. Using a slotted spoon, move the croquettes to a warmed serving dish. Carefully lift and tilt the chicken over the pan to empty any juices from the body and place on a carving board. Once slightly cooled, carve into thick slices.

Heat the roasting pan of cooking juices on top of the stove and stir in the crème fraîche. While stirring, allow the sauce to bubble for about a minute, then season to taste with salt and pepper. Add the feathery part of the fennel, bubble for a minute more and pour into a jug to serve with the slices of roast chicken.

RATATOUILLE
· IN A PORK CASE ·

INGREDIENTS

- 1 aubergine, halved lengthways and thinly sliced
- sea salt and freshly ground black pepper
- 350g fresh plum tomatoes
- 2 tbsp olive oil
- 2 peppers, 1 green and 1 red, seeds and stems removed and roughly chopped
- 1 large onion, roughly chopped
- 2 tsp caster sugar
- butter, for greasing
- plain flour, for dusting

For the pork case:
- 680g pork mince
- 2 large garlic cloves, crushed
- 1 tbsp tomato purée
- 3 tsp wholegrain mustard
- 80g wholemeal flour
- 1 large egg, beaten
- sea salt and freshly ground black pepper

SERVES 6–8

This intrigued everyone when I first presented it and now I am intrigued, as I can't remember how I came up with it! But thank goodness I did.

Cover the aubergine in salt. Set in a colander over the sink for 30 minutes. Rinse thoroughly and pat dry. Make a small cross incision in each tomato and cover with boiling water. Leave for 1–2 minutes, then drain, remove and discard the skin and roughly chop the flesh.

Heat the oil in a large sauté pan over a medium heat. Stir in the aubergines, peppers and onion and fry until soft. Add the tomatoes and cook until softened. Add the sugar and seasoning and remove from the heat. Set aside.

Preheat the oven to 170°C/Gas mark 3. Lightly butter and flour a 21–23cm earthenware flan dish. Put all the pork case ingredients into a mixing bowl and mix until thoroughly combined. Using well-floured hands take just under two-thirds of the meat and place on a lightly floured surface. Use your hands to lightly press the mixture into a circular shape just bigger than the diameter of the flan dish. Carefully line the dish with the meat, pushing it up the sides so that it extends above the rim, making sure there are no gaps. Spoon in the vegetable mixture.

Using the remaining meat mixture, repeat the method above to make a circle the size of the dish. Moisten the edges with water and place on top of the vegetables. Press down the edges so that the meat overlaps – it will shrink slightly as it cooks. Brush with a little oil and place on a baking tray. Bake for ¾–1 hour, or until well browned. Cut into large wedges and serve.

'THE PIG,
IF I AM NOT MISTAKEN,
GIVES US HAM AND PORK AND BACON.
LET OTHERS THINK HIS HEART IS BIG,
I THINK IT STUPID OF THE PIG'

Ogden Nash

CHINESE
• HEDGEHOGS •

- 225g pudding rice
- sea salt
- 500g lean pork mince
- 2 large garlic cloves, finely chopped
- 3cm piece of ginger, peeled and finely chopped
- 50g tinned anchovy fillets, oil reserved
- 225g tin of water chestnuts, in brine, drained
- 2–3 pinches of chilli powder
- 3–4 tbsp cornflour
- 3–4 spring onions, trimmed and very finely sliced
- soy sauce, to serve

SERVES 5–6

The Chinese have thought up some ingenious dishes and this is one that I have adapted to make even simpler. Minced pork and water chestnuts are formed into balls and studded with rice. I call them hedgehogs for obvious visual reasons! You will need to have a large steamer, or bamboo trays that can be stacked up one above the other over a saucepan of bubbling water.

Put the rice in a sieve and rinse thoroughly with cold water. Place the rinsed rice in a bowl of cold salted water to cover and leave to soak for an hour or more.

Meanwhile, in a bowl mix together the pork, garlic and ginger. Add the oil from the anchovies. Finely chop the water chestnuts and anchovies and add to the mince. Season with chilli powder and salt and mix until combined. Shape the mixture into balls about the size of large marbles.

Drain the rice and transfer to a bowl. Place the cornflour in another bowl. Dip the pork balls, one at a time, into the cornflour until coated and then into the rice, patting it on to ensure the balls are completely covered. Place slightly apart in a large steamer or in two layers of a smaller one.

Bring the water in the steamer or saucepan to the boil and reduce the heat to a gentle simmer. Put the tray or trays of hedgehogs over the water, cover and steam for 30 minutes. Gently transfer the hedgehogs to a warmed serving plate and sprinkle with the spring onions and a drizzle of soy sauce.

PORK AND PEAR
• PARCELS •

INGREDIENTS

- 250g lean pork mince
- 1 large garlic clove, finely chopped
- 3cm piece of ginger, peeled and finely chopped
- sea salt and freshly ground black pepper
- 1 tbsp groundnut or sunflower oil
- 1 tbsp soy sauce
- 2 large firm dessert pears
- juice of ½ lemon
- 250g extra thin rashers of smoked and rindless streaky bacon
- 80g wild rocket leaves

SERVES 4

Pears, for a reason I have never been able to explain, are not my favourite fruit, but I have found they work well in savoury dishes. These, stuffed with ginger flavoured pork and wrapped in bacon, are a testament to that. I like them best for a light lunch or supper served with a mixed salad and warm crusty bread.

Place the pork in a bowl with the garlic, ginger and seasoning. Heat the oil in a frying pan over a high heat, add the mince mixture and stir for 5–6 minutes, or until separated and browned. Add the soy sauce and cook for another minute. Remove from the heat and set aside.

Preheat the oven to 180°C/Gas mark 4. Peel the pears, cut them in half lengthways and rub with the lemon juice to prevent discolouration. Carefully cut out the cores, and hollow out a little to form a good-sized cavity. Divide the bacon equally into four and, one portion at a time, lay the rashers out on a flat surface – they should slightly overlap. Set a pear half in the centre of the bacon slices and spoon a quarter of the mince mixture into the hollow of the pear, pressing it down lightly. Don't worry if a little mince tumbles out of the pear and onto the bacon. Carefully bring the bacon up and over to enclose the pear and place in a roasting pan. Repeat with the remaining bacon, pear and mince mixture.

Place the roasting pan in the centre of the oven and cook for 20–25 minutes. Serve immediately or keep warm in a very low oven for up to an hour. To serve, arrange a bed of rocket leaves in a serving dish and spoon the pear parcels and any pan juices over the top.

TAGLIATELLE WITH
· VEAL SWEETBREADS ·

- 250g veal sweetbreads
- sea salt
- 1–2 tbsp white wine vinegar
- 4–5 fresh plum tomatoes
- 25g butter
- 1 tbsp olive oil
- 175g lean veal mince
- 100g small chestnut mushrooms, finely sliced
- 300ml crème fraîche
- 1–2 pinches of chilli powder
- 280g egg tagliatelle
- 12 basil leaves, roughly torn

SERVES 4–5

The melting texture of sweetbreads combined with the rich veal make this a wonderfully creamy, subtly flavoured pasta dish. Veal sweetbreads are superior but you can use lambs, which are cheaper. Serve with a generous sprinkling of freshly grated Parmesan.

Soak the sweetbreads in a bowl of cold, salted water for at least an hour, changing the water two or three times until clear of all traces of blood. Add the vinegar and sweetbreads to a saucepan of boiling water, reduce the heat and simmer for 1–2 minutes. Drain and finely chop.

Make a small incision in each tomato, place in a bowl and cover with boiling water. Leave for a minute or two, then drain. Remove and discard the skin and roughly chop the flesh. Melt the butter with the oil in a large frying pan over a fairly high heat. Add the veal mince and, using a wooden spoon, stir for 1–2 minutes, or until the mince has separated and sealed. Add the chopped tomatoes and mushrooms and cook for 2–3 minutes. Reduce the heat to low and add the sweetbreads. Stir until the sweetbreads are pale and opaque, then add the crème fraîche and allow to bubble for 1 minute. Remove from the heat, add salt and chilli powder and set to one side.

Bring a large saucepan of salted water to the boil, add the tagliatelle and cook until al dente, about 8–10 minutes (the pasta should still have a very slight bite to it). Reheat the sauce if necessary and stir through the basil leaves. Drain the pasta, rinse with hot water and place in a warmed serving bowl. Mix the sauce into the pasta and serve at once.

PORK STUFFED ROLLS
· IN WHITE WINE ·

- 250g pork mince
- 2 large garlic cloves, finely chopped
- 2 sprigs of rosemary, finely chopped
- sea salt and freshly ground black pepper
- 1 tbsp olive oil, plus extra for oiling
- butter, for frying
- 4 large skinless chicken breast fillets
- 1 egg, beaten
- 150ml white wine
- 1 rounded tsp cornflour
- a small handful of flat-leaf parsley, finely chopped

SERVES 4

I have always found whole chicken breasts to be incredibly boring, but sliced and paired with good flavourings they can be wonderfully versatile. These rolls are delectable; coated with a delicate sauce they go especially well with new potatoes and fresh peas.

In a bowl, mix together the mince, garlic, rosemary and seasoning. Heat the oil and a knob of butter in a frying pan and add the pork mixture. Cook over a high heat, while stirring, until the mince has separated and browned, about 5 minutes. Transfer to a dish and leave to cool.

Cut the chicken fillets in half lengthways. Place on a sheet of oiled greaseproof paper, leaving some space between each fillet. Lay another sheet of oiled greaseproof paper over the top and beat the fillets with a rolling pin or mallet until much thinner. Sprinkle with salt and pepper.

Preheat the oven to 190°C/Gas mark 5. Stir the egg into the mince mixture and place a large spoonful on the middle of each chicken fillet. Roll the ends over the stuffing and set in an ovenproof dish, join side down and close together. Press any leftover stuffing onto the ends and pour over the wine. Cover the dish with foil.

Cook the rolls in the centre of the oven for 30–35 minutes, or until opaque. Carefully pour the cooking juices into a small saucepan. Mix the cornflour with a little water to create a smooth paste and add to the saucepan. Bring to the boil. Stir for 2–3 minutes, or until thickened – if the sauce is too thick add a little more wine. Season and add the parsley. Pour over the rolls and serve.

HOTSTUFFED
· AVOCADOS GRATINÉE ·

INGREDIENTS

- 2 red peppers, seeds and stems removed and roughly chopped
- 5 large garlic cloves, skin left on
- 1 tbsp lemon juice, plus extra for coating
- sea salt and freshly ground black pepper
- 2 tbsp olive oil
- 1 red onion, roughly chopped
- 250g pork or veal mince
- 2 tsp dried oregano
- 4 large, firm avocados
- 75g strong Cheddar cheese, grated
- 25g Parmesan, freshly grated

SERVES 4

You may be doubtful at the idea of hot avocados but these are a real treat. Serve with sprigs of watercress and hot crusty bread.

Place the peppers into a saucepan of boiling water with the whole cloves of garlic. Cover the pan, reduce the heat and simmer gently for 10 minutes. Drain the peppers and press the soft garlic out of their skins. Place the peppers, garlic and lemon juice into a food processor and blitz to a smooth purée. Season to taste and set to one side.

Heat the oil in a frying pan over a fairly low heat and fry the onion for 1–2 minutes, or until just softened. Increase the heat and add the mince and seasoning. Stir to break up the mince and cook for 5–8 minutes, or until separated and browned. Add the oregano and the pepper purée and bubble for a minute or two. Remove from the heat. Check the seasoning – it should be quite highly seasoned to combine with the bland avocado.

Preheat the oven to 190°C/Gas mark 5. Cut the avocados in half, remove the stones and smear the flesh immediately with some lemon juice. Place them in a shallow ovenproof dish and spoon the mince mixture into the stone cavities, spreading the rest of it evenly over the top to ensure that all the avocado flesh is covered. Sprinkle the Cheddar and Parmesan on top of the meat and cook in the centre of the oven for 15–20 minutes.

PORK ROLLS IN
· A LEMON SAUCE ·

- 1 tbsp olive oil, plus extra for oiling
- 1 red onion, chopped
- 2–3 large garlic cloves, finely chopped
- 2 rounded tsp ground coriander seeds
- 400g veal mince
- 2 fresh plum tomatoes
- 4–5 pinches of mild chilli powder
- sea salt and freshly ground black pepper
- 400g pork fillets
- 1 egg, beaten
- 300ml hot water
- juice of 1 lemon
- 2 tsp cornflour
- a good handful of flat-leaf parsley, finely chopped

SERVES 6

These delicious little rolls are beautifully tender. Pork fillets are used to wrap a stuffing of veal mince and tomato, enhanced by crushed coriander seeds. For the best aroma always grind whole spices in a pestle and mortar or coffee grinder as and when you need them.

Heat the oil in a large pan over a low heat and fry the onion until soft. Add the garlic and ground coriander and stir for 30 seconds. Increase the heat, add the veal and cook until separated and browned. Lower the heat. Make an incision in the tomatoes, place in a bowl and cover with boiling water. Leave for 1–2 minutes, remove and discard the skin and finely chop the flesh. Add to the pan and cook until dry. Remove from the heat and add the chilli and seasoning. Set aside.

Preheat the oven to 180°C/Gas mark 4. Slice the pork fillets lengthways into 1cm-thick slices. Lay the pieces, well spaced out, onto a sheet of oiled baking paper. Cover with another sheet of oiled paper. Using a rolling pin or mallet bash the fillets until much thinner and 2–3 times their original size. Be careful not to break the fillet. Mix the egg into the mince mixture and evenly spoon onto the middle of the pork pieces. Roll the fillet around the mince and place join side down in a roasting pan. Pour the hot water over the rolls and cover with foil. Cook in the centre of the oven for 45 minutes.

Using a slotted spatula, transfer the rolls to a warmed serving dish. Strain the pan juices into a saucepan and add the lemon juice. Mix the cornflour with a little water and stir into the juices. Bring to the boil and allow to bubble gently for 2–3 minutes. Stir through the parsley and some seasoning and pour over the rolls to serve.

• PORK AND POTATO PIE •

INGREDIENTS

- 680g potatoes, peeled
- 80g butter, plus extra for baking
- sea salt and freshly ground black pepper
- 3 large garlic cloves, roughly chopped
- 1 large egg, beaten
- plain flour, for dusting
- 500g pork mince
- 1 large orange or red pepper, seeds and stem removed and finely chopped
- 75g smoked and rindless bacon, finely chopped
- 2 tsp wholegrain mustard
- oil, for oiling

SERVES 6–7

This is a good family dish, equally popular with adults and children. It is made in a Swiss roll fashion, with mashed potato encasing a pork mixture, full of flavour and baked until crisp and golden.

Boil or steam the potatoes until soft. Put in a mixing bowl, add the butter and some seasoning and mash until smooth. Purée the garlic with a little salt using a pestle and mortar. Stir the garlic purée and egg into the potato and set aside to cool.

Preheat the oven to 180°C/Gas mark 4. Sprinkle a sheet of baking paper or foil generously with flour. Place the pork in a bowl, and stir through the pepper, bacon, mustard and some seasoning. Spoon the potato onto the baking paper and, with floured hands, pat out into an oblong shape about the size of a baking tray. Evenly spread the meat mixture over the potato. With the help of the paper, roll the short end up and over (like a Swiss roll) and continue to roll until all the filling is enclosed. Carefully slide the roll off the paper onto a well-oiled rectangular ovenproof dish. Use a knife to criss-cross the top to make a diamond pattern and dot with butter. Cook in the centre of the oven for 1–1¼ hours, or until a rich golden brown.

STEAMED PORK
· PUDDING ·

- 2 large red peppers, halved lengthways and seeds and stems removed
- 500g lean pork mince
- 2 large eggs, beaten
- 2 tbsp tomato purée
- 2½ tsp whole green peppercorns, in brine
- sea salt and freshly ground black pepper
- butter, for greasing
- 150ml soured cream

SERVES 4–5

When I first made this simple dish I remember being excited by the combination of flavours; a smokiness from the grilled red peppers is mixed with the fresh, sharp and almost fruity taste of green peppercorns. It transforms a meatloaf into something much more special. Mashed potato is a good accompaniment.

Preheat the grill and line the grill tray with foil. Lay the peppers skin side up on the foil and place under the hot grill until blackened all over. Wrap the peppers in foil and leave until cool enough to handle. Remove and discard the skin and chop the flesh as finely as possible.

In a bowl, mix the pork, peppers, eggs, tomato purée, 2 teaspoons of the peppercorns and some seasoning.

Generously butter a 1 litre pudding basin. Spoon in the mince mixture and smooth the top level. Cover the basin with foil and secure with string. Cut another length of string and attach this to the secured string to create a handle. Place the basin in a saucepan and fill with enough hot water to come halfway up the side of the basin. Cover the pan and let the water simmer gently over a low heat (checking now and then to make sure that the water has not boiled away) for 1 hour.

Carefully lift out of the saucepan using the string handle and leave to sit for 5 minutes. Remove the foil and turn out onto a large round plate, so that the pudding is surrounded by its delicious juices. Roughly crush the reserved peppercorns. Just before serving spoon over the soured cream and scatter with crushed peppercorns.

POTATO CROQUETTES
· STUFFED WITH PORK ·

- 1.25–1.5kg potatoes, peeled
- 50g butter
- sea salt and freshly ground black pepper
- 1 tbsp olive oil, plus extra for oiling
- 1 red onion, finely chopped
- 250g pork or veal mince
- 2 large garlic cloves, finely chopped
- 1 rosemary sprig, finely chopped
- 100g Gorgonzola or Saint Agur cheese, crumbled
- 1 tbsp double cream or crème fraîche
- 100g walnut pieces, finely chopped

SERVES 6–8

Always provoking enthusiasm from both adults and children, these croquettes make a good change for a family meal. With a crunchy walnut coating they are stuffed with a scrumptious blending of pork, onion, rosemary and Gorgonzola cheese. Fun to make and easy to cook, these are best served with a rocket and baby tomato salad.

Boil or steam the potatoes until soft. Place in a mixing bowl, add the butter and seasoning and mash until smooth. Set aside.

Heat the olive oil in a frying pan over a low heat, add the onion and fry gently until soft. Increase the heat, stir in the mince and cook until separated and browned all over. Add the garlic and leave for 1–2 minutes. Transfer to a bowl and stir in the rosemary. Add the Gorgonzola cheese, cream and seasoning and combine.

Take small handfuls of the potato mash and form into balls, each about the size of a large plum. Use your thumb to create a good pocket in the centre of the ball and spoon in a heaped teaspoonful of the mince mixture. Lightly press the potato around the mixture to enclose it. Repeat until all the mixture is used up.

Preheat the oven to 190°C/Gas mark 5. Smear the potato balls with olive oil and then roll them lightly in the chopped walnuts. Place them close together in a large, shallow ovenproof dish. Cook in the centre of the oven for 35–45 minutes, or until golden brown.

PORK, RED ONION AND COURGETTE TART

INGREDIENTS

- 1 large garlic clove, finely chopped
- 250g pork mince
- sea salt and freshly ground black pepper
- 25g butter
- 1 tbsp olive oil
- 450g small red onions, thinly sliced into rings
- a small handful of mint leaves, finely chopped
- 500g courgettes, trimmed
- 300ml crème fraîche
- 2 eggs, plus 2 egg yolks
- ¼ whole nutmeg, grated

For the pastry:
- 225g strong plain flour, plus extra for dusting
- ½ tsp salt
- 100g cold butter, cut into cubes, plus extra for greasing
- 50g cold lard or vegetable fat, cut into cubes
- 1 cold egg
- 2 tbsp cold water

SERVES 6–8

This is wonderfully creamy and best when hot. The old-fashioned pairing of butter and lard makes the pastry deliciously crumbly, but use vegetable fat if you prefer.

For the pastry, sift the flour and salt into a bowl. Add the butter and lard and use your fingers to crumble into rough breadcrumbs. Mix the egg with the water, and, using a knife, stir into the mixture. With floured hands, gather into a ball, wrap in cling film and refrigerate for 30 minutes.

Preheat the oven to 220°C/Gas mark 7. Butter a deep 21–23cm diameter loose-based tin. On a floured board, roll the dough out larger than the base of the tin. Line the tin with the dough, pushing it just above the rim. Prick the base with a fork and refrigerate for 30 minutes.

Cover the pastry with a piece of baking paper. Fill the tin with baking beans and bake blind in the oven for 10–15 minutes, or until the pastry is a pale brown. Remove the beans and paper and return to the oven for 5–8 minutes, or until a golden brown. Remove from the oven and turn the heat down to 190°C/Gas mark 5.

Mix together the garlic, pork and seasoning. Heat the butter and oil in a frying pan over a medium heat. Add the onions and pork and cook until the meat has separated and browned. Remove from the heat and stir in the mint.

Cut the courgettes into narrow strips, about 7.5cm long. Plunge into boiling salted water for 1 minute, drain and set aside. Whisk the crème fraîche, eggs, nutmeg and seasoning. Spoon the pork mixture into the pastry case and spread level. Arrange the courgettes in a pattern and pour over the egg mixture. Cook in the centre of the oven for 25–35 minutes, or until the cream is lightly set.

LAMB

SPICYLAMB
· PIES WITH CAPERS ·

INGREDIENTS

- 2 tbsp groundnut or sunflower oil, plus extra for oiling
- 2 tsp ground cinnamon
- 1 tsp ground turmeric
- 1 tsp cumin seeds
- 1 red pepper, seeds and stem removed and finely chopped
- 2 fresh plum tomatoes, roughly chopped
- 250g lean lamb mince
- 1–2 small red chillies
- 3 large garlic cloves, finely chopped
- 1 tsp small capers
- sea salt and freshly ground black pepper
- 375g packet of puff pastry

SERVES 4–6

These puffed up little pies are perfect for a light lunch, a supper with a leafy green salad or, as they can be made ahead and re-heated, a party. The pies must be served hot for the best aroma and crispness.

Heat the oil in a large frying pan over a medium heat. Add the spices and stir around for a few seconds, then add the pepper, tomatoes and the lamb. Increase the heat and fry for 8–10 minutes, stirring until the meat has separated and browned and any liquid has evaporated. Cut the chillies open lengthways under running water, remove the stem and seeds and slice the flesh thinly. Stir the chillies, garlic, capers and seasoning into the meat. Turn the meat mixture out into a bowl and leave to cool.

Preheat the oven to 220°C/Gas mark 7. On a lightly floured surface, roll out the pastry until about 5mm thick. Brush a 12-hole patty or muffin tin with oil. Use a 7.5cm diameter pastry cutter to cut out 12 circles and then use a 6.5cm cutter to cut out 12 further circles. Line the tins with the larger circles and spoon in the cooled meat mixture, filling them to the top. Now moisten the edges of the smaller circles and lay them on top of the filled pies, pressing the edges to seal. Cut a small slit in the centre of each pie and brush the tops with oil. Bake for about 15 minutes in the centre of the oven or until a golden brown.

ONION AND YOGURT SODA BUNS STUFFED WITH SPICED LAMB

INGREDIENTS

- 1 tbsp groundnut or sunflower oil, plus extra for oiling
- 2 large garlic cloves, finely chopped
- 1 tsp paprika
- 1 tsp ground cinnamon
- 1 tsp cumin seeds
- 250g lean lamb mince
- sea salt
- 2–3 pinches of mild chilli powder

For the dough:
- 350g strong white or brown flour, plus extra for dusting
- 1 tsp fine sea salt
- 2 tsp bicarbonate of soda
- 2 tsp cream of tartar
- 2 red onions, finely chopped
- 6 tbsp whole milk yogurt
- 250ml milk, plus extra
- 1 egg yolk

SERVES 6–8

Everyone loves these, and they take hardly any time to make. They are perfect for picnics or a quick lunch. If you want to make them in advance for a picnic, wrap them in foil and carry them in an insulated food bag.

Heat the oil in a frying pan over a medium heat. Stir in the garlic, paprika, cinnamon and cumin seeds and cook for 1 minute. Add the lamb mince, increase the heat and stir around with a wooden spoon for 3–4 minutes, or until separated and browned. Remove from the heat and season to taste with salt and chilli powder. Transfer the mixture to a bowl and set aside to cool.

To make the dough, sift the flour, salt, bicarbonate of soda and cream of tartar into a bowl and stir in the onions. Mix the yogurt with the milk and add to the flour mixture. Stir until the dough comes together. The dough should be quite sticky so add a little more milk if necessary. Turn the dough out onto a well-floured surface and using floured hands, knead lightly for 2–3 minutes, or until smooth. Preheat the oven to 200°C/Gas mark 6.

Take a small amount of the dough and shape it into a ping-pong sized ball. Flatten it with the palm of your hand to create a flat round and pile 2 teaspoons of the lamb mixture into the centre. Bring the sides of the dough up to enclose the meat and create a parcel. Lightly roll it around in your hands to form a ball again. Continue like this until you have used up all the dough and all the mince mixture. Place the filled buns a little apart on a large, lightly oiled oven tray. Mix the egg yolk with a little milk and brush the tops of the buns to create a glaze. Cook in the centre of the oven for 20–25 minutes, or until golden brown.

ATLAS MOUNTAIN
·SOUP·

- 2 tbsp olive oil
- 2–3 large garlic cloves, finely chopped
- 2 tsp ground cinnamon
- 1 tsp ground turmeric
- 2 tsp cumin seeds
- 2 tsp paprika
- 500g lean lamb mince
- 100g dried apricots
- 4 celery sticks, trimmed and cut into small pieces
- 1 large red pepper, seeds and stem removed and sliced into thin strips
- 500g fresh plum tomatoes, roughly sliced
- 1 lemon
- 400ml pure apple juice
- sea salt and freshly ground black pepper
- plain yogurt, for serving (optional)

SERVES 4–6

It was a trip through the Atlas mountains of Morocco in 1970 that inspired this family standby. I love good homemade soup for a simple weekend lunch when the damp winter chill begins, one that served with warm crusty bread is sustaining enough as a meal on its own. This substantial lamb and vegetable soup is just that, and includes the characteristic flavours of Moroccan food – cinnamon, cumin, apricots and lemon.

Heat the olive oil in a fairly large and heavy casserole dish over a gentle heat. Add the garlic, cinnamon, turmeric, cumin seeds and paprika and stir around for no more than a minute. Immediately mix in the lamb mince, increase the heat and using a wooden spoon, stir the meat until separated and browned. Add in the apricots, celery, red pepper and tomatoes.

Cut 10–12 strips of zest from the lemon and extract its juice. Stir the lemon zest, lemon juice and apple juice into the casserole mixture and season to taste. Bring to the boil, cover, lower the heat and leave to simmer gently for 30 minutes. If you like you can spoon a little yogurt into each bowl of hot soup just before serving.

CRISPY LAMB
AND MINT ROLLS

INGREDIENTS

- 350g lean lamb mince
- 3 large garlic cloves, finely chopped
- 3–4cm piece of ginger, peeled and finely chopped
- 2 tsp ground cumin
- ¼–½ tsp of mild chilli powder
- sea salt
- olive oil, for frying
- a handful of mint or coriander leaves
- 1 large egg, lightly whisked
- 375g packet of puff pastry
- groundnut oil, for deep-frying

SERVES 6–8

Flavoured with mint, ginger and cumin these rolls are far more interesting than sausage rolls and are perfect for a dinner party canapé or as part of a lunch. They can be made in advance and kept warm or reheated. Serve with a bowl of whole milk yogurt for dipping.

In a large bowl, mix together the lamb, garlic and ginger. Stir in the cumin and chilli powder and season with salt. Heat some olive oil in a large frying pan and add the lamb mixture. Fry the meat over a high heat, using a wooden spoon to continuously stir the meat until it has separated, browned and any liquid has evaporated. Transfer the lamb to a bowl and leave until completely cold.

Chop the majority of the mint, reserving a few leaves to garnish, and stir into the cold meat mixture with the egg. On a lightly floured surface, roll out the pastry into a long strip, about 65 x 20cm. Slice in half lengthways. Spoon the meat mixture evenly over both strips, making sure all the pastry is covered. Then press the meat down firmly. Carefully roll the pastry strips over widthways, to create what will look like a long thin Swiss roll. Press all along the width end of the pastry to seal. Slice the roll at 6.5cm intervals to create small pastry swirls.

Fill a large, deep, heavy-based sauté pan with enough oil to deep-fry the rolls in a single layer. Place over a high heat and when it is very hot add about half of the rolls. Fry for a few minutes until puffed up and golden brown. Remove from the pan using a slotted spatula and place on absorbent kitchen paper to drain off any excess oil. Repeat with the remaining rolls. Serve piled on a serving dish, scattered with the reserved mint leaves.

LAMB AND AUBERGINE DOME WITH A
· TOMATO SAUCE ·

- 2 tbsp white wine vinegar
- sea salt and freshly ground black pepper
- 500g aubergines, peeled and sliced into 1cm thick rounds
- 1 tbsp olive oil, plus extra for oiling
- butter, for frying
- 2 onions, finely chopped
- 350g lean lamb mince
- 50g feta cheese, crumbled
- 50g walnut halves, roughly chopped
- 2 large eggs, beaten
- 1 tbsp sesame seeds

For the sauce:
- 4–5 fresh plum tomatoes
- 1 tbsp olive oil
- 25g butter
- 2 tbsp sun-dried tomato purée
- 4 tbsp water
- 1 tsp caster sugar
- sea salt and freshly ground black pepper

SERVES 6

I love lamb with aubergine, a combination that evokes memories of the time I spent in both Syria and Turkey. First brought to America by German immigrants and often used to stretch limited budgets during the Great Depression, meatloafs exist in countless variations.

Fill a large saucepan with water, add the vinegar and a sprinkling of salt and bring to the boil. Add the aubergine and boil for no more than 2 minutes, just until they begin to soften. Drain, finely chop and put to one side.

Heat the olive oil and a knob of butter in a frying pan and fry the onions until soft and golden. Remove from the heat and set aside. Place the lamb in a mixing bowl and use a wooden spoon to mix and pound the meat. Mix in the aubergine, onions, feta, walnuts, eggs and seasoning.

Preheat the oven to 190°C/Gas mark 5. Smear a shallow, round ovenproof dish lightly with oil and spoon the lamb mixture into the centre of the dish. With dampened hands shape the meat into a dome shape, smear all over with a little more oil and sprinkle with the sesame seeds. Cook in the centre of the oven for 1 hour.

Using a sharp knife, make a little incision in each tomato and cover them with boiling water. Leave for a minute or two, then drain. Peel off and discard the skin. Roughly chop the flesh. Heat the olive oil and butter in a heavy saucepan, add the tomatoes and stir over the heat for a minute or two. Then add the tomato purée, water, sugar and a good seasoning of salt and pepper. Cover the pan and simmer as gently as possible for about 30 minutes. Pour the sauce into a jug and keep warm until ready to serve with the lamb and aubergine dome.

MOUSSAKA with
• GRUYÈRE CHEESE •

- 25g butter
- 2 red onions, roughly chopped
- 500g lean lamb mince
- 1 tsp ground cinnamon
- sea salt and freshly ground black pepper
- 2 tbsp tomato purée
- 6 tbsp water
- 600g aubergines, peeled and sliced into 1cm thick rounds and smeared with lemon juice to prevent discolouration
- a handful of flat-leaf parsley, finely chopped
- 100g Gruyère cheese, thinly sliced

For the topping:
- 50g butter
- 50g plain flour
- 500ml whole milk
- a little grated nutmeg
- sea salt and freshly ground black pepper
- 2 egg yolks
- 2 tbsp crème fraîche

SERVES 6

I tasted my first moussaka in the 1960s at a cheap student restaurant in London, before I had ever been to Greece. Everyone seemed to call it Greek Shepherd's pie. The variations are infinite; for this personal version I avoid the time-consuming and oil-absorbing frying of the aubergines. Make well in advance and reheat.

Heat the butter in a large frying pan over a gentle heat, add the onions and cook until just softened. Add the lamb, increase the heat and dig around with a wooden spoon until the meat has separated and lightly browned. Stir in the cinnamon and some seasoning. Add the tomato purée and water and cook until the water has been absorbed. Remove from the heat and set aside.

Bring a saucepan of salted water to the boil. Add the aubergine slices and boil for 2 minutes. Drain, rinse the slices with cold water and pat dry with kitchen paper.

Preheat the oven to 180°C/Gas mark 4. Stir the parsley into the lamb. In a 1.5–1.7 litre capacity ovenproof dish (preferably one that is transparent) arrange, in layers, some aubergine, then some mince, a few Gruyère slices and repeat. End with a layer of aubergine.

To make the topping, melt the butter in a saucepan, remove from the heat and stir in the flour using a wooden spoon. Gradually stir in the milk and bring to the boil, stirring all the time. Bubble gently, still stirring, for about 3 minutes. Add the nutmeg and seasoning. Remove from the heat. Whisk the egg yolks with the crème fraîche and stir into the milk mixture until smooth. Pour over the aubergine and bake in the oven for about 45 minutes, or until a rich golden brown.

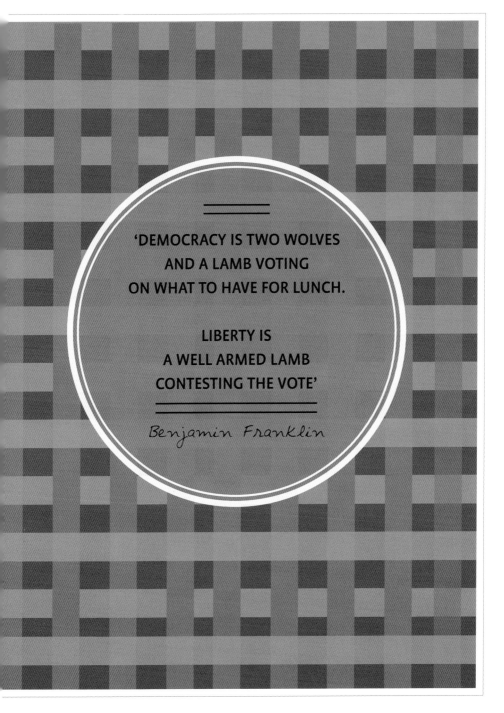

'DEMOCRACY IS TWO WOLVES
AND A LAMB VOTING
ON WHAT TO HAVE FOR LUNCH.

LIBERTY IS
A WELL ARMED LAMB
CONTESTING THE VOTE'

Benjamin Franklin

· SPRING LAMB PIE ·

- 2 tbsp olive oil, plus extra for frying
- 675g lamb fillet or lean lamb mince
- 2 large garlic cloves, finely chopped
- 2 tsp caraway seeds
- 1 tsp ground cinnamon
- sea salt and freshly ground black pepper
- 500g fresh beetroot, cooked, peeled and sliced into 0.5–1cm rounds
- 450–550g potatoes, sliced into 0.5–1cm rounds

For the sauce:
- 5 tbsp cornflour
- 300ml milk
- 300ml soured cream
- juice of 1 lemon
- sea salt and freshly ground black pepper

SERVES 6–8

Perhaps the title of this dish should have been Russian Lamb Pie as it includes many of the characteristic flavours of Russian cuisine: beetroot, soured cream, caraway seeds and cinnamon. At any rate, although the flavours are very sophisticated it will still please both adults and young children alike.

Heat some olive oil in a large frying pan over a high heat. Using a food processor, coarsely mince the lamb fillet. Add the meat to the pan, digging and stirring with a wooden spoon until the mince has separated and browned all over. Lower the heat and add in the garlic and spices. Continue stirring for another minute or two or until any liquid has evaporated. Season well. Turn into a large ovenproof gratinée dish and spread level. Arrange the beetroot slices so that the meat is covered.

For the sauce, place the cornflour in a saucepan and mix to a smooth paste with 4 tablespoons of the milk. Gradually stir in the remaining milk and whisk in the soured cream until smooth. Bring to the boil while stirring constantly. Once it begins to bubble, continue stirring for 3 minutes then remove from the heat. Gradually stir in the lemon juice, then season to taste. Pour the thick sauce evenly over the beetroot slices. Preheat the oven to 190°C/Gas mark 5.

Put the potato slices into a bowl and coat with the oil and a little salt. Place them higgledy-piggledy on top of the sauce. Bake the pie in the centre of the oven for 1–1¼ hours until browned and the potatoes feel soft when you insert a sharp knife or skewer. Serve immediately or keep warm in a low oven until needed.

MONGOLIAN MANTI
WITH A TOMATO SAUCE

Manti are an ancient Mongolian dish, known in Turkey as a sort of dumpling. When I first tasted them in Istanbul I knew I had to try to reproduce them.

- 225g plain flour, plus extra for dusting
- 1 tsp sea salt
- 1 egg, lightly whisked
- 4–5 tbsp water
- 350g lean lamb mince
- 1 red onion, coarsely grated
- a handful of flat-leaf parsley, finely chopped
- sea salt and freshly ground black pepper

For the sauce:
- 500g fresh plum tomatoes
- 50g unsalted butter
- 1 large garlic clove, finely chopped
- 1 tsp caster sugar
- sea salt and freshly ground black pepper
- a small handful of basil leaves, roughly torn

SERVES 6–8

Sift the flour and salt into a mixing bowl. Make a well and add the egg. Fold the flour into the egg using a wooden spoon and gradually add the water until you have a non-sticky dough (you may not need to use all the water). Use floured hands to gather the dough into a ball and knead on a floured surface for 5–8 minutes, or until smooth and pliable. Cover with cling film and leave to one side to rest.

Place the lamb in a mixing bowl and add the onion and parsley. Season with salt and pepper and mix thoroughly. Transfer the dough to a well-floured surface. Roll it out as thin as you can without it tearing. Using a sharp knife, cut into 4–5cm squares. Take one of the squares and spoon a little of the meat mixture into its centre. Moisten the edges with water and fold one side of the dough over the filling to make a triangle. Pinch the edges to seal and lay to one side. Repeat until all the mince has been used.

Bring a saucepan of salted water to a rapid boil. Gently add the manti, cover and simmer gently for 15 minutes. Use a slotted spoon to transfer the manti to a colander. Rinse with hot water and place in an earthenware dish. Cover with foil and keep warm in a low oven.

Make an incision in each tomato and cover with boiling water. Leave for 1–2 minutes, then drain, peel and discard the skin and chop the flesh. Heat the butter in a deep sauté pan and add the tomato and garlic. Simmer gently for 10–15 minutes, or until soft. Stir in the sugar, seasoning and basil and pour over the manti to serve.

CHICKEN & TURKEY

CLEAR CHICKEN BALL
• AND WATERCRESS SOUP •

- 275g skinless chicken breast fillets, cut into chunks
- 2 sprigs of tarragon, finely chopped
- juice and finely grated zest of 1 lemon
- sea salt and freshly ground black pepper
- 1 egg white
- 2 x 400g tins chicken consommé or clear homemade chicken stock
- 300ml water
- a bunch of watercress

SERVES 4

If you're on a low fat diet then this is a treat that you can really indulge in, and as it is so pretty and easy to make it will prove a perfect first course for any occasion. White balls of chicken delicately flavoured with lemon and tarragon float amongst watercress leaves in a clear lemony consommé – lovely!

Using a food processor, blitz the chicken until you have a fine mince. Put the chicken into a mixing bowl with the tarragon and lemon zest. Season well and beat in the egg white using a wooden spoon. With wet hands, form the mixture into about 20 very small balls.

Empty the consommé into a large saucepan and add the water. Using a fine sieve, strain in the lemon juice. Bring the liquid to a rapid boil, then drop in the chicken balls and leave to cook for 4–5 minutes.

Meanwhile, pick the leaves off the watercress stems. Discard the stems and stir the watercress leaves into the soup at the last moment. Immediately remove the pan from the heat and serve.

CHICKEN AND MUSHROOM ROULADE

INGREDIENTS

- 75g butter, plus extra for greasing
- 275g skinless chicken breast fillets
- 1 large garlic clove, finely chopped
- 2 tbsp plain flour
- 300ml whole milk
- sea salt and freshly ground black pepper
- 50g chestnut mushrooms, finely sliced
- 2 sprigs of tarragon, stalks discarded and leaves chopped
- 50g Parmesan, freshly grated

For the batter:
- 25g butter
- 40g plain flour
- sea salt
- 1 large egg, lightly whisked
- 150ml whole milk

SERVES 4–5

The combination of chicken and tarragon is heavenly. This dish is easy as you only need to make one big pancake and cook it in the oven. Filled with creamy chicken, this dish is simple, impressive and irresistible!

To make the batter, melt the butter in a saucepan and then cool by sitting the pan in cold water. Sift the flour and a pinch of salt into a bowl. Add the egg and a little milk and whisk. Continue to whisk while adding the remaining milk and just before you have added it all mix in the melted butter. Whisk until the batter becomes really smooth. Stand for about 30 minutes.

Preheat the oven to 240°C/Gas mark 9. Butter a roasting tray measuring 33 x 23cm. Put the tray on the top shelf of the oven, leave for a few minutes to get hot, then pour the batter into the tray and cook for 10 minutes until risen and golden. Turn the pancake out onto a flat surface, cover with a clean damp cloth and leave to cool. Turn the oven down to 180°C/Gas mark 4.

Place the chicken in a food processor and briefly blitz until coarse. Melt 50g of the butter in a heavy-bottomed saucepan over a medium heat and add the chicken and garlic. Cook for 3–4 minutes. Add the flour and gradually stir in the milk. Bring to the boil. Lower the heat and, while stirring, simmer for 2–3 minutes. Remove from the heat and leave to cool. Stir in the mushrooms and tarragon.

Spread the chicken mixture over the pancake and roll to create a loose Swiss roll. Butter a large ovenproof dish and carefully lay the roll join side down. Smear the top with the remaining butter and cover with Parmesan. Cook on the centre shelf of the oven for 20–30 minutes.

STEAMED TURKEY BALLS
• SCARLET SAUCE •

- 675g skinless turkey or chicken breast fillets
- 25g fresh white breadcrumbs
- 2–3 sprigs of rosemary, finely chopped
- ¼ whole nutmeg, grated
- 3 tbsp freshly grated Parmesan
- 25g soft unsalted butter
- 1 egg, whisked
- sea salt and freshly ground black pepper
- a handful of basil leaves

For the sauce:
- 1 red pepper
- 25g butter
- 1 tbsp olive oil
- 2 large garlic cloves, finely chopped
- 225g fresh plum tomatoes, finely chopped
- 400g tin of chopped tomatoes
- 2 tbsp tomato purée
- sea salt
- 2–3 pinches of mild chilli powder

SERVES 6

Perfect for those who want to cut down on their consumption of red meat, these meatballs (which can be made with chicken) provide an excellent and delicious alternative. And they have the added health bonus of being steamed rather than fried. Lightly spiced with nutmeg and flavoured with rosemary and Parmesan, they are wonderful covered with the red pepper and tomato sauce.

Blitz the turkey in a food processor until finely chopped. Transfer to a bowl. Add the breadcrumbs, rosemary, nutmeg, Parmesan, butter and egg and mix thoroughly using a wooden spoon. Using damp hands, form the mixture into ping-pong sized balls and lay in the top of a steamer over gently simmering water. Cover and leave to steam for 20–25 minutes, or until opaque in colour.

Meanwhile, make the sauce. Cut the pepper in half, discard the seeds and stem and place in a food processor. Chop as finely as possible. Heat the butter and olive oil in a saucepan over a medium heat, add the garlic and the pepper and its juices and stir for a minute or so. Stir in the fresh tomatoes and cook for a few minutes until mushy. Add in the tinned tomatoes and tomato purée. Cover the pan and simmer gently for about 15 minutes. Remove from the heat and season to taste with crushed sea salt and chilli powder.

To serve, pile the turkey balls onto a warmed serving dish and cover with the scarlet sauce. Roughly tear the basil leaves and scatter over the dish.

CHICKEN, VEAL AND
· SWEETBREAD TERRINE ·

INGREDIENTS

- 225g lamb or calf sweetbreads
- sea salt and freshly ground black pepper
- 225g veal or pork mince
- 350g skinless chicken breasts, minced or finely chopped
- 25g shelled pistachio nuts or cashew nuts, roughly chopped
- 1 tsp green peppercorns, in brine and drained
- 150ml double cream
- butter, for greasing

SERVES 6–8

This pâté is easy to make but has a truly luxurious, delicate and subtle flavour. Serve it on crisp salad leaves as a first course or as part of a cold meal.

Soak the sweetbreads for an hour in several changes of cold salted water to get rid of any traces of blood. Use your hands to remove as much of the fine skin as you can, but don't worry if there is a little remaining. Roughly chop the sweetbreads and put in a mixing bowl with all the other ingredients. Season generously with crushed salt and some pepper and mix together thoroughly.

Preheat the oven to 150°C/Gas mark 2. Half-fill a large roasting pan with hot water and place it just below the centre of the oven. Butter a 900ml earthenware terrine or china soufflé dish and spoon in the pâté mixture. Smooth level and place the dish in the roasting pan of water. Cook for 1¾–2 hours; if the top becomes too brown during cooking, loosely cover the dish with foil for the remaining time. Cool completely and refrigerate before serving.

PESTO PASTA WITH CHICKEN AND PORK MEATBALLS

- 1 large red pepper
- 250g skinless chicken breast fillets
- 350g lean pork mince
- 2–3 large garlic cloves, finely chopped
- a handful of basil leaves, finely chopped
- sea salt and freshly ground black pepper
- 2 tbsp olive oil
- butter, for frying
- 50g pine kernels
- 400g spaghetti or tagliatelle
- 1 tbsp extra virgin olive oil
- 2 rounded tbsp green pesto
- freshly grated Parmesan, for serving

SERVES 6

Despite all my years of cooking meatballs none of my family or close friends seem to tire of them. But such are the possibilities for variation that I hardly ever make exactly the same meatballs twice; these are a recent addition to my very long list.

Heat the grill to its highest setting. Cut the pepper in half lengthways, remove the seeds and stem and lay the halves, skin side up, on a large piece of foil very close to the top of the grill. When the pepper has blackened all over, enclose in the foil and leave to cool. When cool enough to handle, peel and discard the skin and finely chop the flesh. Place the chicken fillets in a food processor and blitz until finely chopped. Turn out into a bowl and add the pork, garlic and basil. Stir until evenly mixed and season well with salt and pepper.

With dampened hands, form the chicken mixture into small meatballs – they should be about the circumference of a 10 pence piece. Heat the olive oil and a knob of butter in a large frying pan over a medium heat. Add the meatballs and fry for 10–15 minutes, turning them so that they are brown all over. Use a slotted spoon to transfer them to a bowl and keep warm in a low oven. Place a large serving dish into the oven to warm up.

Toss the pine kernels briefly in a small dry pan over a high heat until just brown and set to one side. Boil the pasta in plenty of salted water until just tender. Drain and transfer to the warmed serving dish, stirring in the extra virgin olive oil as you do so. Roughly mix in the pesto, pine kernels and the meatballs. Serve with a sprinkling of Parmesan.

TURKEYSTUFFED
· MUSHROOMPUFFS ·

INGREDIENTS

- 500g turkey breast fillets, roughly chopped
- 2 red chillies
- 50g butter, plus extra for greasing
- 25g plain flour, plus extra for dusting
- 270ml whole milk
- 75g whole hazelnuts
- 2 sprigs of tarragon, stalks discarded and leaves chopped
- 100g frozen petit pois
- sea salt
- 250g packet of puff pastry
- 4 very large Portobello mushrooms, stalks removed
- 1 egg yolk

SERVES 4

People find this recipe very intriguing; a creamy turkey (or you can use chicken) mixture, flavoured with chilli and tarragon, studded with hazelnuts and stuffed into mushrooms, then wrapped in pastry. The result is four exciting golden parcels.

Place the turkey in a food processor and finely chop. Slice the chillies in half lengthways under running water, discard the seeds and stems and finely chop the flesh. Melt the butter in a saucepan and stir in the chillies. Add the turkey and coat with the butter, then stir in the flour and gradually add the milk. While stirring, bring the mixture to the boil. Once boiling turn the heat down to a gentle simmer. Cook for 10 minutes, stirring frequently. Remove from the heat and add the hazelnuts, tarragon, petit pois and salt. Turn out into a bowl and set aside until cold.

Grease a baking tray with butter. On a lightly floured surface, roll out the pastry very thinly into a large square, about 30 x 30cm. Cut into 4 squares. Lay each mushroom top side down on a square of pastry and spoon a quarter of the turkey mixture onto the top of each one. One at a time, bring the corners of the pastry up and over the filling. The pastry should meet at the top, enclosing the filling. Moisten the edges with a little water and, leaving small gaps at the bottom corners to allow cooking juices to run out, press to seal. Lay on the baking tray and place in the fridge for 20 minutes.

Preheat the oven to 220°C/Gas mark 7. Brush with egg yolk and cook in the oven for about 20 minutes or until a rich golden brown. Using a spatula, transfer to serving plates, letting any liquids run off.

OPEN SESAME
· ON EMERALD SAUCE ·

This very healthy family dish will keep everyone guessing. To this day nobody has been able to fathom exactly what it is they are eating. A roasted sesame encrusted roll is in fact delicately spiced chicken mixed with chickpeas. And the bright green sauce is simply a purée of courgettes and parsley. Despite its mystery, everyone is always ecstatic about the taste.

Briefly blitz the chicken and chickpeas in a food processor and transfer to a mixing bowl. Add the garlic, ground coriander, caraway seeds, butter and seasoning. Use a large wooden spoon to stir the mixture until combined. Don't worry if there is some unblended butter. Add the egg whites and breadcrumbs and stir well.

Preheat the oven to 220°C/Gas mark 7. Lightly cover your hands and a board with olive oil. Take up all the chicken mixture and shape it into a 15cm long, fat sausage shape. Press the sesame seeds all over the meat until densely coated. Place in a large, oiled roasting pan and cook on the middle shelf for about 15 minutes, or until browned. Turn the heat down to 180°C/Gas mark 4 and continue to cook for 1 hour.

Towards the end of the roasting time make the sauce. Roughly cut the courgettes into chunks. Boil or steam for a few minutes, or until just tender. Place in a food processor with the butter, parsley, nutmeg and seasoning. Blitz to a soft purée. Spoon into a warmed serving dish. Place the sesame roll on a chopping board and, using a sharp knife, slice across into 5mm–1cm slices. Arrange the slices on top of the green sauce and serve.

INGREDIENTS

- 500g skinless and boneless chicken thighs
- 420g tin of chickpeas, drained
- 3 large garlic cloves, finely chopped
- 2 tsp ground coriander seeds
- 2 tsp caraway seeds
- 75g butter, softened
- sea salt and freshly ground black pepper
- 2 egg whites
- 50g fresh brown breadcrumbs
- olive oil, for oiling
- 50g sesame seeds

For the sauce:
- 1kg courgettes, trimmed
- 100g unsalted butter, cut into pieces
- a handful of flat-leaf parsley, roughly chopped
- ¼–½ whole nutmeg, freshly grated
- sea salt and freshly ground black pepper

SERVES 4

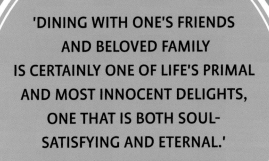

'DINING WITH ONE'S FRIENDS
AND BELOVED FAMILY
IS CERTAINLY ONE OF LIFE'S PRIMAL
AND MOST INNOCENT DELIGHTS,
ONE THAT IS BOTH SOUL-
SATISFYING AND ETERNAL.'

Julia Child

· HUNTER'S PIE ·

- 2 wood pigeons, flesh removed and bones discarded
- 350g skinless and boneless chicken thighs, roughly chopped
- 250g veal mince
- 2 tsp green peppercorns, in brine and drained
- 50g tinned anchovy fillets, oil drained
- 2 tsp wholegrain mustard
- 8–10 juniper berries, crushed
- 10–12 sage leaves, roughly chopped
- 150ml soured cream
- sea salt and freshly ground black pepper
- a little milk

For the pastry:
- 350g strong plain white flour, plus extra for dusting
- 1 tsp salt
- 225g unsalted butter, plus extra for greasing
- 2 tbsp water
- 1 egg, beaten

SERVES 8–10

This is rather like a game pie; eaten cold, it is perfect for parties, accompanied by hot new potatoes. During autumn and winter most butchers sell wood pigeon but you can use a small guinea fowl if you can't find them.

Briefly blitz the pigeon and chicken in a food processor. Mix with the veal, peppercorns, anchovy fillets, mustard, juniper berries, sage, soured cream and seasoning.

To make the pastry, sift the flour and salt into a bowl and make a well. In a saucepan, gently melt the butter with the water and pour into the flour. Stir until evenly mixed, add the egg and continue mixing vigorously until you have a smooth dough. Gather into a ball and set aside to cool. Butter a deep, 20cm cake tin with a spring base.

Split the pastry in two; you need a large ball made up of three-quarters of the dough and a small ball made from the remaining dough. On a floured surface, roll the small ball until slightly bigger than the cake tin base. Place the tin on top and cut around the edge to make a perfect circle. Set aside. Lightly dust the work surface. Using the large ball, roll out a circle large enough to line the bottom and sides of the tin, about ¼cm thick. Transfer to the tin and press lightly into the corners and sides. Spoon in the meat mixture. Fold the edges of pastry over the filling and moisten. Sit the smaller round of pastry on top and press to seal. Cut 2–3 small incisions in the top and decorate with trimmings. Put in the fridge for 1 hour.

Preheat the oven to 180°C/Gas mark 4. Brush with milk and cook for 1½–1¾ hours, or until a rich golden brown. If it starts to burn, cover with foil. Leave to cool. Ease the edges and push the pie out of the tin. Serve in slices.

TURKEYROLLS
· INASPINACHSAUCE ·

- 350g skinless turkey breast fillets
- 100g soft white cheese
- 1 large egg yolk
- a bunch of chives
- sea salt and freshly ground black pepper
- 8 large, thin slices of good quality honey roast ham
- olive oil, for oiling
- 500g large leaf spinach, stalks removed and roughly chopped
- 25g unsalted butter
- 2 tbsp fresh orange juice

SERVES 4

Simple, pretty and delectable – when I first made this my greediest daughter said, 'Oh please, give me more and more.' The delicate flavours and clear colours compliment each other beautifully and if you serve this with baby carrots it will look even more attractive.

Preheat the oven to 180°C/Gas mark 4. Half-fill a large roasting tray with hot water and place just below the centre of the oven. Blitz the turkey breast in a food processor. Put in a bowl with the cheese and egg yolk and mix thoroughly. Use scissors to finely chop the chives into the mixture and season.

Lay the slices of ham out onto a flat surface and spread an even amount of turkey mixture towards one end of each piece. Roll the ham over to enclose the mixture and create a Swiss roll shape. In an ovenproof dish, arrange the rolls so that they sit close together in a single layer. Smear with some oil and cover loosely with foil. Place the dish in the middle of the large roasting tray of water and cook in the oven for 1 hour.

Pour the cooking juices into a large saucepan and return the covered dish to the switched off oven. Bring the juices to the boil and add the spinach. Cover the pan and bubble for a few minutes, or until the spinach wilts. Stir in the butter and orange juice and remove from the heat. Season to taste with plenty of pepper and, if needed, some salt, and purée in a food processor until smooth. Spoon the sauce over the rolls just before serving.

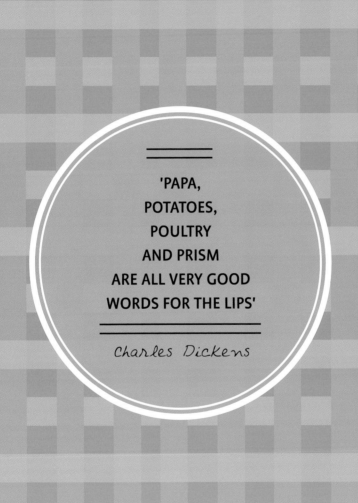

'PAPA,
POTATOES,
POULTRY
AND PRISM
ARE ALL VERY GOOD
WORDS FOR THE LIPS'

Charles Dickens

TURKEY BALLS WITH LEMON AND CARDAMOM

- 350g skinless turkey or chicken breast fillets
- 50g fresh white breadcrumbs
- a small bunch of spring onions, trimmed and finely chopped
- finely grated zest of 1 lemon
- 8–10 cardamom pods
- 1 egg, beaten
- 3–4 pinches of mild chilli powder
- 1–2 tsp sea salt
- butter, for frying
- 1 tbsp groundnut or sunflower oil
- 200ml crème fraîche
- a handful of coriander leaves, roughly chopped

SERVES 4–5

At the start of the 1980s cardamom was an unfamiliar spice in the United Kingdom. I started experimenting with it in both savoury and sweet dishes after I fell in love with its unique and versatile flavour on my first trip to India in 1977 – I always feel, and hope, that I helped to promote it in this country. This recipe is perennially popular, both for its delicate flavour and because it is so quick and easy.

Roughly chop the turkey fillets and blitz in a food processor until coarsely minced. Place in a bowl with the breadcrumbs, spring onions and lemon zest. Make a small incision in the cardamom pods and remove the seeds. Grind the seeds finely using a pestle and mortar or electric coffee grinder. Add to the turkey mixture with the egg, chilli powder and salt. Use dampened hands to form the mixture into balls about the size of large marbles.

Heat a knob of butter and oil in a large frying pan over a fairly gentle heat, add the balls and fry, turning frequently, for 15 minutes, or until lightly golden brown. Transfer to a warmed serving dish. Heat the crème fraîche and pour over the turkey balls. Sprinkle with coriander and serve.

CHICKEN LIVER, BACON
• AND AUBERGINE PIE •

INGREDIENTS

- 2 large aubergines, about 550g
- sea salt and freshly ground black pepper
- 180g smoked and rindless back bacon
- 225g chicken livers
- 4 tbsp crème fraîche
- 1 tsp dried oregano
- 100g chestnut mushrooms, roughly chopped
- butter, for frying
- olive oil, for frying
- 1 large onion, finely chopped
- 25g fresh white breadcrumbs

SERVES 5–6

Related to both the Shepherd's pie and to moussaka, but without the beef or lamb, this soft textured and richly flavoured dish is loved by all who enjoy comfort dishes. I like it best served with a mixed leaf salad.

Slice the aubergines into 1cm rounds, rub with salt and leave in a colander over the sink for at least 30 minutes to allow any bitter juices to drain away. Finely chop the bacon and chicken livers and place in a bowl. Stir in the crème fraîche, oregano and mushrooms.

Heat a knob of butter and a tablespoonful of oil in a large frying pan over a fairly low heat and fry the onion gently, stirring now and then, until soft and transluscent. Mix the onion into the liver mixture and season with plenty of pepper and a little salt.

Thoroughly rinse the salt off the aubergine slices and pat dry using absorbent kitchen paper. Add a knob of butter and 2 tablespoons of olive oil to the frying pan and fry the aubergine over a fairly high heat until golden brown on both sides. You may need to cook these in 2 or 3 batches. Drain the cooked slices on kitchen paper.

Preheat the oven to 190°C/Gas mark 5. Place half the aubergine slices on the bottom of a fairly deep, 20cm round ovenproof dish. Add the liver mixture and cover with the remaining aubergine. Sprinkle with breadcrumbs and evenly drizzle with olive oil. Cook in the centre of the oven for 25–30 minutes, or until golden brown.

FISH

· SESAME BITES ·

- 350g cod or haddock fillets, skinned
- 6–8cm piece of ginger, peeled and cut into small pieces
- 1–2 red chillies
- 4–5 cardamom pods
- 2 large garlic cloves, roughly chopped
- 1 rounded tsp sea salt
- a large handful of coriander leaves, roughly chopped
- 1 egg, lightly whisked
- 50–70g sesame seeds
- groundnut oil, for roasting
- 2 tbsp lemon juice

For the sauce:
- 300g plain whole milk yogurt
- 3–4 tsp tikka paste
- 2 tsp lemon juice

SERVES 4

These bite-sized treats are aromatic and crunchy, and delicious served with the yogurt sauce. Serve them as a hot first course or as a light lunch with a good mixed salad. They can be made in advance and reheated or kept warm for up to an hour in a low oven.

Mix all the ingredients for the sauce together. Spoon into a serving bowl and place in the fridge until needed.

Blitz the cod in a food processor until mushy. Transfer to a bowl. Use a garlic press to squeeze the juice from the ginger onto the fish and discard the pieces of ginger. Cut the chillies in half lengthways under running water and remove all the seeds and the stems. Slice the flesh into thin strips and stir into the fish. Make a small incision in the cardamom pods and extract the seeds. Grind the seeds to a fine powder using a pestle and mortar and pound the garlic and salt to a purée. Stir both into the fish along with three-quarters of the coriander and the egg.

Preheat the oven to 190°C/Gas mark 5. Spread the sesame seeds out onto a flat surface. With dampened hands, take up small handfuls of the mixture and form into small balls. Roll the balls in the sesame seeds until completely coated. Oil the bottom of a roasting pan and arrange the balls in one layer. Spoon a little oil over the top of each and bake in the centre of the oven for 20–25 minutes. Remove from the pan using a slotted spoon and place in a serving dish. Stir the lemon juice into the pan juices and spoon over the fish balls. Sprinkle with the remaining coriander and serve with the spiced yogurt dip.

MOUSSELINES
• IN A PEA SAUCE •

INGREDIENTS

- 225g smoked cod fillets, skinned
- 100g Gruyère cheese, finely grated
- ¼ whole nutmeg, finely grated
- 3 large eggs, separated
- 3 tbsp double cream
- sea salt and freshly ground black pepper
- plain flour, for dusting
- 225g podded peas, fresh or frozen
- 300ml whole milk
- a handful of flat-leaf parsley, finely chopped

SERVES 4

A dreamy dish: smoked fish, Gruyère cheese and egg white are combined and poached to produce lightly puffed, irregular shaped balls, served in a pea and parsley sauce. Perfect for a light summer lunch when served with new potatoes, sliced tomatoes and a drizzle of good quality olive oil.

Blitz the cod in a food processor until very finely chopped; it should be mushy in consistency. Keep the food processor running and add the cheese, the nutmeg, the egg whites a tablespoon at a time and finally the cream. Season and turn the mixture out into a bowl.

Preheat the oven to 150°C/Gas mark 2. Bring a large saucepan of salted water to the boil. Flour a flat surface. Take teaspoons of the fish mixture and push them off the spoon and onto the dusted board. Roll until lightly covered with flour and place on a plate. Drop them into the water and gently boil for about 3 minutes. Remove from the heat. Carefully lift the mousselines out of the water using a slotted spoon. Place in a serving dish, cover loosely with foil and keep warm in a low oven.

Cook the peas, drain and rinse with cold water. Place in the food processor with the egg yolks and milk. Blitz until smooth. Pour into a saucepan and heat gently without allowing it to come to the boil. Stir constantly until thickened, about 5 minutes. If the sauce curdles, blitz it in the food processor and return it to the pan. Stir in the parsley, pour over the mousselines and serve.

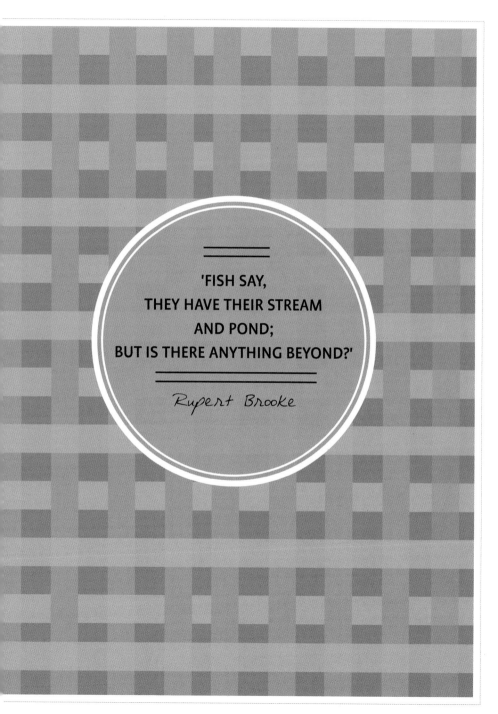

'FISH SAY,
THEY HAVE THEIR STREAM
AND POND;
BUT IS THERE ANYTHING BEYOND?'

Rupert Brooke

QUENELLES WITH
· A SAFFRON SAUCE ·

- 270ml whole milk
- 10–15 strands of saffron
- 400g naturally smoked haddock or cod fillets, skinned
- 2 large eggs, separated
- 1 tbsp chopped fennel or dill
- 3–4 pinches of mild chilli powder
- 4 Torbay sole, dab or plaice fillets, skinned
- olive oil, for oiling
- 1 tbsp cornflour
- 30ml dry Vermouth
- sea salt
- a handful of flat-leaf parsley, for serving

SERVES 4

I developed a passion for quenelles on my first trip to France, aged six, and I have never stopped loving the way these almost melt in my mouth. This variation is a delicate, mouthwatering dish, ideal for summer.

Preheat the oven to 200°C/Gas mark 6. Heat the milk in a small saucepan until it begins to boil, then remove from the heat. Add the saffron strands and set aside to infuse.

In a food processor, finely chop the smoked fish and mix in the egg whites. Transfer to a mixing bowl and stir in the fennel and a pinch of chilli. Lay the sole fillets out on a lightly oiled flat surface. Divide the smoked fish mixture into 4 and pat into fat sausage shapes. Place a sausage onto the middle of each fish fillet and roll up loosely. Place in an ovenproof dish join side down and brush with oil. Place in the centre of the oven for 15–20 minutes, or until the fish becomes opaque.

Meanwhile, make the sauce. Add the cornflour and 2 tablespoons of the saffron infused milk into a saucepan over a low heat and stir to a smooth paste. Add the remaining milk and saffron strands. Gradually bring to the boil, stirring constantly. Once it begins to bubble gently, cook for 3–4 minutes, or until thickened. Remove from the heat and briskly whisk in the egg yolks. Stir in the Vermouth and season with salt and a pinch of chilli.

When the fish is cooked, pour the cooking juices into the sauce and stir thoroughly. Pour over the fish, scatter with parsley and serve.

· FISHSAUSAGES ·

- 500g cod or haddock fillets, skinned
- 2 large eggs, separated
- 15g cornflour
- 1 tsp baking powder
- sea salt and freshly ground black pepper
- 2–3 pinches of mild chilli powder
- finely grated zest of 1 orange
- 50g butter
- 1 tsp paprika
- 25g plain flour
- 500ml whole milk
- 100g Red Leicester cheese, coarsely grated
- a bunch of spring onions, trimmed and finely chopped

SERVES 4–5

In a bid to entice my children, I called these fish sausages instead of quenelles. It worked. They adored them, and the cheese sauce went so well with another of their favourites, broccoli. All this is not to say that this isn't a dish for adults – it's comfort food for all.

Put the skinned fish in a food processor with the egg whites, cornflour and baking powder. Season with salt and chilli and blitz until a smooth paste. Stir in the orange zest. With wet hands, take up bits of the mixture and pat into small, fat sausages. Bring a large saucepan of water up to a rolling boil. Drop in the sausages and simmer for 7 minutes. Drain gently into a large colander or remove from the water with a slotted spatula. Arrange the sausages in a shallow ovenproof dish.

Preheat the oven to 150°C/Gas mark 2. In a saucepan, melt the butter with the paprika. Remove from the heat and, using a wooden spoon, stir in the flour until a smooth paste. Gradually stir in the milk, return to the heat and, stirring constantly, bring to the boil. Allow the mixture to bubble gently, while still stirring, for about 3 minutes, or until thickened. Stir in the cheese and egg yolks. Season to taste and add the spring onions. Pour over the fish sausages. Place the dish in the centre of the oven for 25–30 minutes.

Heat the grill to its highest setting. Place the dish under the grill for 2–4 minutes, or until the top is speckled with dark brown patches.

SMOKED FISH
· IN TURKEY BREASTS ·

- 350g smoked cod fillet, skinned
- 75g fresh white breadcrumbs
- 1 rounded tsp chopped dill, plus extra to serve
- finely grated zest of 1 lemon
- 2 eggs, separated
- sea salt and freshly ground black pepper
- olive oil, for oiling
- 450g skinless turkey breast fillets, cut into 6 equal pieces
- butter, for greasing
- 150ml soured cream
- 2 tsp tomato purée

SERVES 6

This looks skilled but is simple to do; turkey fillets are beaten until thin and wrapped around smoked cod to form parcels. The combination of delicate flavours and textures is delicious. It's a great spring or summer dish.

Using a food processor, coarsely mince the smoked cod. Transfer to a mixing bowl and add the breadcrumbs, dill and lemon zest. Mix together using a wooden spoon. Add the egg whites and season well. Stir until combined.

Preheat the oven to 190°C/Gas mark 5 and butter an ovenproof dish. Place a large piece of oiled greaseproof paper onto a flat surface. Lay the pieces of turkey, well spaced out, onto the paper and lay another piece of oiled paper on top. Using a rolling pin or mallet, bash the fillets until much thinner and larger. Remove the top sheet of paper. Spoon an equal amount of the fish mixture into the middle of each piece. Bring one side of the turkey fillet up and over the filling to enclose it – don't worry if there are small gaps. Lay the parcels join side down in the ovenproof dish; they should fit in one layer. Cover with foil.

Cook in the centre of the oven for 30 minutes. Pour any cooking juices into a saucepan off the heat and return the parcels to a switched off oven. Add the soured cream, tomato purée and egg yolks to the cooking juices and stir until smooth. Place the pan over a gentle heat and stir constantly without allowing to bubble for 3–5 minutes, or until the sauce is thick enough to coat the back of a metal spoon. Remove from the heat and season. Pour the sauce over the turkey parcels and sprinkle with a little dill.

SMOKED HADDOCK
· MOUSSE ·

- 100g butter, plus extra for greasing
- 125g peeled prawns
- 500g smoked haddock fillets, skinned
- 3 large eggs, separated
- 300ml double cream
- 3–4 pinches of mild chilli powder
- sea salt
- 300ml whole milk
- 8–12 strands of saffron
- 1 level tbsp plain flour
- 1 tsp tomato purée
- 2 sprigs of dill, finely chopped, plus extra for serving
- 2–3 tsp white wine vinegar

SERVES 4–5

This is easy to make and has a delicate flavour that combines luxuriantly with the buttery sauce. Serve simply with a mixed leaf salad for the ultimate treat.

Preheat the oven to 180°C/Gas mark 4. Half-fill a roasting pan with hot water and place in the oven. Generously butter a 1 litre ring mould, a round cake tin or 4 individual metal moulds. Distribute 25g of the prawns in the mould. In a food processor, blitz the haddock fillets with the egg whites until finely chopped. Add the cream and season with chilli powder and salt. Spoon the mixture into the mould and spread level. Place in the pan of water and return to the oven. Cook for 20–25 minutes, or until it feels firm when lightly pressed.

Meanwhile, make the sauce. Add the milk and saffron to a saucepan. Bring to the boil, then remove immediately from the heat. In another saucepan, melt 25g of the butter. Remove from the heat and using a wooden spoon stir in the flour until smooth. Gradually stir in the saffron-infused milk and return to the heat. While stirring, bring to the boil. Allow the sauce to bubble for 2–3 minutes, or until thick and smooth. Cut the remaining 75g of butter into small pieces and stir into the sauce one at a time. Mix in the egg yolks, tomato purée, dill, vinegar and the remaining 100g of prawns. Season to taste with salt and chilli powder and transfer to a serving jug.

The mousse can be kept warm for up to 25 minutes in a switched off oven. To serve, loosen the edges of the mousse carefully using a palette knife. Turn out into a serving dish, pour over the sauce and garnish with dill.

· SALMON FISHCAKES ·

- 350g salmon fillets, skinned
- 75g fresh white breadcrumbs
- 100g hard goat's cheese, grated
- a bunch of spring onions, trimmed and finely sliced
- sea salt
- 4–5 pinches of mild chilli powder
- 1 egg, plus 1 egg yolk
- plain flour, for dusting
- butter, for frying

SERVES 4

I have made many versions of these light, potato-free fishcakes over the years. They are ideal for a light meal or even a first course. Serve with a really good mayonnaise flavoured with some chopped dill.

Briefly chop the salmon in a food processor; be careful not to over-process as you don't want it to be too finely minced. Place in a mixing bowl with the breadcrumbs, goat's cheese and spring onions. Season with salt and the chilli powder and mix together using a wooden spoon. Whisk the egg and extra yolk together and stir into the mixture. With well-floured hands, shape the mixture into 8 fairly small fishcakes and dust with flour until completely covered.

Heat a good knob of butter in a large frying pan. Fry the fishcakes over a medium heat – you'll probably have to do them in two batches – for a few minutes. Using a spatula, flip the fishcakes and fry for a few more minutes on the other side. They are cooked once they are a lovely golden brown. Transfer the fishcakes to a warmed dish, pour over any butter from the pan and serve immediately.

INDEX

ACKNOWLEDGEMENTS

I shall always be grateful to John Sainsbury for having the idea that I should be the first person to write cookbooks for Sainsbury's and to the team at Sainsbury's for telling me at the start of the 1980s that the ingredient they sold most of was 'mince'; hence giving me the inspiration for what became a bestseller and something of a cult book – *Marvellous Meals with Mince*.

I also owe heartfelt thanks to my family and friends who were the first to try so many of my mince creations while I worked on the first edition of this book, and still appear to be appreciative today when I make yet more versions of meatballs or Shepherd's pie.

I am indebted to Steven Joyce for his sparkling contemporary photographs of my dishes, and to Louise, Nikki, Ros, Helen and Leonie at Quadrille who helped make this revised and expanded new edition look so stylish. Special gratitude must go to Jane O'Shea who realised that it was high time that *Marvellous Meals with Mince* reached an even wider audience.